Life After Layoff

The Lilac Layoff

Life After Layoff

Six Proven Courses of Action

Richard J. Van Ness, Ph.D.
&
Edith M. Donohue, Ph.D.

All Rights Reserved
Copyright © 2009

Richard J. Van Ness, Ph.D. & Edith M. Donohue, Ph.D.

BookSurge Publishing

Editor
Mary H. Van Ness

Life After Layoff
Six Proven Courses of Action

ISBN 1-4392-4510-X
Library of Congress Control Number 2002109938

Printed in the United States of America

To order additional copies, please contact us.
www.booksurge.com
Toll free at 1-866-308-6235

No part of this book may be reproduced or transmitted in any form or by any means, graphic, electronic, or mechanical, including photocopying, recording, taping or by any information storage or retrieval system, without permission in writing from the authors.

Neither the authors nor the publisher is engaged in providing legal, investment, accounting, or other such services. If this sort of expert advice is desired, be sure to consult with a competent professional person.

To my wife Mary and our sons Richard J., Jr., Michael P. and Robert K.

To my husband Sam and our daughters, Kathy and Debbie

*Destiny is not a matter of chance, it is a matter of choice;
it is not a thing to be waited for,
it is a thing to be achieved.*
—William Jennings Bryan

Table of Contents

Table Listing..xi
Foreword...xiii
Introduction..1

CHAPTER ONE
Assess the Present
    Introduction..7
    The Rumor Mill 8
    The Formal Communication System............................9
    Inevitable Change or Self-fulfilling Prophesy?..........10
    Dealing With It..11

CHAPTER TWO
Strengthen Self Awareness
    Introduction..25
    Don't Shoot the Messenger 25
    Problems, Challenges, and Opportunities.................27
    Alternative Courses of Action 28
    Dealing With It..39

CHAPTER THREE
Utilize Financial Tools

    Introduction 41
    The Long-Range Forecast 41
    Circumstances 46
    Damage Control 47
    How Will I Manage? 48
    Interim Business 55
    Moving On 57

CHAPTER FOUR
Highlight Your Many Values

    Introduction 63
    The Marketing Mix 64
    You as the Product 64
    Your Self-Promotion 71
    Your Place 82
    Your Price 84

CHAPTER FIVE
Learn from Others

    Introduction 103
    Your Options 103
    Decision Making Process 104

CHAPTER SIX
Prepare for a Soft Landing When a Layoff is Imminent

    Introduction 121
    Zephyr Before the Storm 122
    On-the-Job Behavior 122
    A Note on Education 126
    Another Note on Education 127

   Surviving the First Round 128
   Tightening the Financial Belt....................................130
   Job Search Assistance...137

CHAPTER SEVEN
Pull It All Together
   Introduction..139
   Navigating Through the Perils..................................139
   A Safe Harbor...141
   What Lies Ahead? 149
   The Biggest Job Market Threats 150
   Forecasted Job Opportunities...................................150
   Resource Center...153

EPILOGUE
Some Final Thoughts 163

Acknowledgements

Thanks to my students who are transitioning from one career to another who were willing to share details of their difficult journeys and their discovery of pathways to success in this tumultuous economy.
Richard J. Van Ness

Thanks to Lee Richmond, Ph.D. for her teaching which prepared me for the work, her mentoring which gave me the competence and her support that gave me the confidence. And a special thanks to all my clients for sharing their life stories with me and allowing me the privilege to assist them on their career path.
Edith M. Donohue

Table Listing

2-1	Value Systems
3-1	Reasons for Extended Mass Layoffs
3-2	Fastest Job Growth Prospects by Job Title
3-3	Largest Job Growth Prospects by Job Title
4-1	"Product" Self-Analysis
4-2	Promotion—Windows of Opportunity
4-3	Work Force Populations—Specific Groups
4-4	Questions to Answer for a New Place Decision
4-5	Your Price
4-6	Worksheet for Compensation Package Analysis 1
4-7	Worksheet for Compensation Package Analysis 2
4-8	Questions to Answer for Job Planning
5-1	Analyze the Data
6-1	Actions to Extend Employment When Layoff is Imminent
6-2	Job Training Offered by Most Organizations
6-3	Correlation of Unemployment Rate, Education Level, and Median Earnings
6-4	Tough Choices
6-5	The Do's and Don'ts of Tightening the Financial Expenditures Belt
6-6	More Job Search Web Addresses
7-1	Employee Compensation

Foreword

There was a time when people were fired only because of incompetence or the inability to do their job because of extenuating circumstances. Today competent, bright, accomplished employees are being laid off. Companies are closing, merging, relocating, buying up or out. Workers from CEO's to front line staffers are being notified. There is no longer a formula for work that guarantees employment. Additionally, outside forces have caused an impact on our lives and lifestyles. The tragic events of September 11, 2001, in New York City, Pennsylvania and Washington, D.C. resulted in the loss of many human lives. The dark shadow of those events was cast over our nation and our socio-economic system of everyday life. Beyond the obvious tragedies, the attacks exacerbated certain already weakened economic conditions and resulted in more thousands of layoffs.

Life after Layoff, provides the knowledge, understanding, tools and strategies to manage a career during these turbulent times. It appears that the current unsettled employment environment is here to stay. This is not necessarily bad news. It is just news; the way it is. The best approach is to accept this situation, rather than fight it or feel overwhelmed. Tens of thousands of workers have successfully transitioned from apparent security to unemployment, then re-employment, only to find themselves repeating the cycle once again.

One of the greatest fears of those unemployed is the financial challenge. It is a time for caution and cutting back. However, it does not have to result in a lessening of potential wealth and prosperity. In fact, a new job or new business opportunity may increase chances for accumulating wealth. Remember, the millionaire next door achieved that status by living within his or her means, no matter what those means were at different times of life.

Financial security begins with an attitude of desire and recognition of the realities of the moment. When laid off, life choices and plans must be readjusted. Unemployment does not necessarily predict an erosion of your wealth. There are ways, to manage money and lifestyle choices, which will assure stability. With the budget assistance presented in this book, confidence and stability can be regained. Maintenance of wealth at this time requires sacrifice, but the pay off is worth the temporary adjustment of purchasing strategies.

This book can provide a road map for traveling a new career path. There may be a concern that the unemployment situation is unmanageable, but there are proven strategies for successful re-employment. The book includes stories of people who have improved their financial situation and found more satisfying work. These stories provide real life examples of how others have succeeded. Indeed, such people are loving life after layoff.

Hundreds of survivors were interviewed to learn how they adapted and moved beyond the momentary set back of lay off. These experienced survivors provide some models of behavior and choice that can help anyone who is willing to invest the time and energy in using the six proven strategies outlined in this book. No one wants

Foreword

to search for all the answers on his or her own. Taking advantage of the reports from others will ease the transition back to gainful work. This book brings the reader remedies that have worked for others. There are many kinds of examples to choose from; assuredly there will be a story for everyone.

Examination and practical application of the methods for not only surviving, but also thriving in the world of work after lay off are here for the willing.

The reflection and self-assessment, required to carefully plan strategies, provide a deeper understanding of skills and interests. Values clarification can strengthen the ability to find ways to work, people to work with, and settings that support the best work. Accomplishments provide a higher level of satisfaction when values are met at work.

Clearly stating personal qualities, experiences that describe best past accomplishments, and what increases enjoyment in service to others, can prepare the job searcher to take what initially appears to be a set back and turn it into opportunity. It is possible to create a life that best suits skills and talents acquired over a lifetime. Finding the right placement adds an element of joy in daily life. Discover that one can do what is loved and get paid in the process.

Success, happiness, and fulfillment is conceivable. Successful survivors may even become mentors to others, in this way sharing the knowledge and experience of achievement.

Reading this book is not enough. Action must be taken. Following the methods offered and using all the support systems available will ensure the attainment of successful work and life style.

Drs. Van Ness and Donohue have done a fine job

outlining the challenges and rewards obtainable to those in transition. Use this well researched advice to move your life forward to success, happiness, and financial security.

William D. Danko, Ph.D.

Introduction

News of extended layoffs is a recurring event. If you are impacted with such news in the form of a job dismissal, the total number of workers affected by the layoff, whether it is 300, 2,000, or 6,000, is not relevant to you. What really matters is how you will deal with your serious situation. Each person will react to the unfortunate news in his or her own way. Our book is about providing individuals with better choices that are summarized into six courses of action.

This book is based on extensive research in the human resource profession. We have two prime missions. First, and most importantly, is to help those who have been dismissed from their jobs, and second, to help those who may be on the firing line take steps for a strategic move before the cut.

During the nineties a layoff was referred to as: employee outplacement, downsizing, rightsizing, reengineering, the offering of a career transition opportunity, repositioning, releasing redundant workers, elimination of employment security, or thrusting employees into a career change opportunity. Today we're back to employees being fired, canned, or axed. If it happens to you, no matter how it is presented, you no longer have a job. You are unemployed. Tomorrow you cannot go to work.

How are you going to deal with that?

No matter what change was going on in your organization, the effect is the same to you. Out of work! Our book will give you some steps to follow to get yourself back on track. We will give you practical advice on how to handle the emotional aspects of job loss. Further, we will offer advice on urgent issues, such as rearranging your finances. Let us walk with you through this process, and as we go along, we will tell you some stories about others who have had a similar experience. Knowing how they worked through the problems and succeeded will give you the courage to move ahead. These stories will also show you that you are not alone, and that you too, can take an experience that may at first seem loaded with failure, and turn it around to your benefit.

Some of you reading this book may actually have been hoping that the axe would fall. However, now that it has actually happened, you may still be facing some tough challenges in making this event work for you.

As you read through the chapters, keep in mind that we are presenting a process, not just a set of suggestions. Each chapter will be addressing a stage in your journey from unemployment to reemployment, whatever that may mean to you. You may be seeking paid work, full or part-time, volunteer opportunities, or maybe you want to start your own business. No matter what your goal is, you will find help in our approach.

Chapter 1
Assess the Present

Chapter 1 will review what brought you to the present or impending situation or predicament. How your company handled the notification will affect how you feel about your circumstances. You need to be aware of how you are feeling about what happened. Take the time to acknowledge those feelings and reactions and learn how to use them to reinforce your energy.

Chapter 2
Strengthen Self Awareness

Chapter 2 will help you to identify and evaluate alternatives. You need to be aware of your emotions, dreams and real barriers. This is an opportunity for you. You will do some reflection on your history and learn how to use your natural gifts and talents to find the kind of work you want.

Chapter 3
Utilize Financial Tools

Chapter 3 will give you tools for planning. You will gather data and take a pragmatic look at the economic reality of your present situation. Then you will be guided through an easy-to-understand financial planning system. Your financial "portfolio" will help you to build a bridge to the future by using tested techniques that work.

Chapter 4
Highlight Your Many Values

Chapter 4 takes the show on the road. You must be able to describe yourself with accuracy and energy. This is where you will learn truth in marketing. If you have never boasted about your accomplishments before, it is now time to do so. You will learn why your resume must be the closest to perfection that you will ever become.

Chapter 5
Learn from Others

Chapter 5 provides you with practical suggestions on how to actually land your next job opportunity. We will give you advice from those who have traveled the path and secured what they wanted.

Chapter 6
Prepare for a Soft Landing
When a Layoff is Imminent

Chapter 6 offers proactive suggestions to help you avoid a crash landing. We examine on-the-job behaviors, financial considerations, and the pursuit of alternative employment *before* unemployment.

Chapter 7
Pull It All Together

Chapter 7 explains how to keep what you have intact. We will show you how to be in charge of your own career path. You will learn how to use your knowledge about yourself to continue to make choices that move you forward on your purposeful path. A safe harbor is created by you, not the world around you. You will see how the skills you develop in managing a career change that you have not chosen, will give you the confidence and ability to face the future. You will have the assurance that you can handle the shifts that life may hand you.

The data you collect about yourself, after a thorough assessment, gives you the navigational ability to chart the rapids before and during your run through them. Life is a mix of quiet and rough waters. Most experience more white water than smooth. Acknowledging this and then preparing for it will give you strength and fortitude.

Chapter One

> **ASSESS THE PRESENT**
>
> ❧❧❧
>
> **Course of Action Number 1**

Introduction

Chapter 1 will review what brought you to your impending situation or predicament. How your company handled the notification of job loss will, without a doubt, affect how you feel about your circumstances. You need to be aware of how you are feeling about what happened. Take the time to acknowledge those feelings and reactions, and learn how to use them to reinforce your energy.

You will have the opportunity to review the flow of feelings, beginning with shock, which is usually followed by fear, and then anger. Denial usually comes on the heels of anger, after which you begin to negotiate. Acceptance is considered the final stage, although an individual may cycle or recycle through any or all of these phases during the process.

You will be introduced to others who have experienced these stages. Their stories will illustrate what you may also encounter.

There are many resources available to you through your organization, community and educational institutions. You will want to know where to go for assistance and support.

🙶 🙶 🙶

The Rumor Mill

The rumors have been rampant for the last few weeks. Every time one of the managers gets called upstairs and returns with messages about reorganizing and budget cuts, your anxiety heightens. Despite assurances that no decisions have been made, you still wonder how long until the shoe drops.

During all of this time, you will experience a range of responses, from anger, to disbelief, to relief. That will depend largely on the kinds of communication channels established in the company. If information is not provided, people will likely make up stories! It is exhausting to maintain productivity and a sense of balance if rumors are flying and management is not keeping the employees informed.

🙶 🙶 🙶

The Formal Communication System

Some organizations will keep all parties apprised. Company newsletters, memos and regular meetings are often used to try to contain rumors and reassure employees. Veterans of layoffs report that both formal and informal communication systems have their up and down sides. There is accuracy to the belief that all rumors have some truth. It is hard to tell when the full truth lives in a rumor. It can be a warning, if nothing else. Formal systems do keep you informed, but can also raise fear and anxiety.

Not knowing is frightening, but sometimes knowing that the axe will fall is also scary. Look for the truth wherever it appears and learn to separate fact from fiction.

Consider talking with the staff in Human Resources. Keep in mind that if a layoff is imminent they are the people who will be implementing the program. Some of their jobs may also be on the line, so expect some concern among the HR staff. They may not be permitted to reveal much information.

Your supervisor or manager is another potential source of truth. Consider exploring your worries and ask for some clarification.

Check the business section of your local newspaper. Reporters often have information and write stories in the papers before formal notification occurs. If your company trades publicly on a stock exchange, keep an eye on stock prices. You don't have to be an investor! Look for fluctuations in stock price and articles that might give you clues. Traditionally there was an inverse relationship between bad news for employees (layoffs) and good news for investors (stock price increases). However, more recently there seems to be mutual pain sharing by employees and investors.

❧ ❧ ❧

Inevitable Change or Self-Fulfilling Prophesy?

While all this upheaval is part of a process, remember that your job performance may negatively or positively affect the situation. Not just you, but all the employees. Often organizations look at several possibilities for restructuring and layoff is only one option among many. You can be sure that during this time of appraisal, productivity and profits will be scrutinized carefully and often.

During this period tension is high, performance may decline and you may notice that other employees take more sick leave. Stress can cause illness or an inability to cope. This is not the time to slow productivity. Time and attendance factors will probably be under investigation. Employees need to take care of themselves so they do not get sick. If you have an Employee Assistance Program (EAP) in your company, consider contacting a counselor for advice on how to handle stress. Avoid making the workplace situation worse so that a reduction of employees is inevitable, when in fact it may presently be just an option. Each individual makes an impact, so be careful of any consequences your actions may incur.

This book is all about how to handle yourself throughout your current situation. Just keep in mind that you operate in a society where every action you take

Assess the Present

results in a reaction. You can control your behavior. If you are a positive "voice," your behavior can influence others. Perhaps your energy and attitude will help others. You can be a model of good coping skills. Unfortunately, you can do all the right things and still wind up with a pink slip or a notification of job termination.

Dealing With It

You have been notified! You no longer have a job. No matter how your organization delivered that bad news the outcome is still the same; you are unemployed.

How you receive the message will set the stage for your future actions. Acknowledge your emotions. Allow them to surface. Today many corporations retain consultants to train managers on the finer points of the "notification meeting." This preparation is designed to give you, the exiting employee, support and information. But, if you are a veteran of the event, you know that much of what is said to you at that time is, at best, fuzzy logic. What you recall is that you no longer have a job; and probably HOW the message was delivered.

Shock:

You will be in shock. It can last from a few minutes, to several hours, to a few days, or a week. Any longer period is unhealthy. You will be unable to grasp the meaning of what has just happened. You may appear to be in perfect control to others. It will seem that you are handling the news well, but what is really going on is that you are in a temporary state of anesthesia. It is a passing escape. Your mind closes down and refuses to deal with the reality.

After hearing of her job loss, the accountant calmly cleared out her desk and headed home. When her husband and the kids were at dinner, she made her announcement with no emotion. Although her family was surprised, they did not discuss the situation for long because of her cool manner. She was having all sorts of turmoil in her mind as well as her body at this time. She had a splitting headache, upset stomach, and was feeling almost detached, but she believed that the best course of action was to hide all this from her loved ones. By doing this, she did not allow them to give her support and to give vent to her feelings. The feelings were there, but just not showing.

They erupted the next day when she was unable to stop crying and spent the entire day in bed almost paralyzed. Not being honest about what was going on only delayed the reaction and when she most needed support, she was home alone.

In another case, the man who lost his construction job just could not face up to telling his family. He dressed and left for "work" at the usual time. For several days, he went to the movies, races and the library to hide out until it was time to go home. He just showed up as if nothing had happened. Finally, he told his wife what had happened. Naturally, she was upset and angry that he had not been truthful from the beginning. So, instead of her support, he was on the receiving end of a harsh tirade. When he most needed support, he denied himself by deceiving his wife. And, when the news came out, he now had to deal with her anger as well as his own emotions.

Assess the Present

Fortunately, this sense or condition of unreality does not last long. The mind is giving you time to come to grips with the truth. The best thing to do is to enlist someone immediately to help you through the trauma. Your company might provide a counselor to meet with you after you have been notified. The company may even schedule a workshop on self-assessment and the job search. The staff in Human Resources may be available to answer your questions or just offer moral support.

Scenario 1-1

Shock: Client Case

At an electronics company, several employees were notified that their jobs were ending. It came as no surprise to most of them as the company had been very truthful about the upcoming reorganization. The affected employees knew which departments were affected and many had scheduled job interviews before the notification. However, there was one young woman who broke into tears and was unable to talk to anyone. She was led, tissues in hand, to the office of the outplacement counselor who let her cry it out. After a few minutes, the young woman caught her breath and said, "I just can't believe it!" The counselor took the woman's hand and said, "I'll bet you are really relieved." She straightened up in her chair, smiled and said softly, "You're right!" Once she had a few minutes to deal with the blow, she recovered and went on to talk about how she really hated her job and was thrilled not to have to come back the next day. She called the counselor the following morning to say she had cried all the way home—with happiness.

There are no magic potions or spells to move you beyond shock. It requires the passage of time and sometimes the words of another to bring you back to the real world. Just be aware that if you find yourself wandering around in a daze, it is not a sign of mental illness! It is a natural reaction. But once you are aware, it is time to get a grip. Then you will better understand your next reaction.

Fear:

No job. No income. No place to go. No identity. Loss of pride and self-esteem. What's next? These are scary issues.

You must go home and let your family or friends know what happened. You wonder what they will think, how they will act. You begin to "awfulize." You could lose your house, your car, your ability to pay the bills . . . and what about your kids? The list will mount depending on your lifestyle. How much you have in savings, your spouse's job situation, and your total debt will all come crashing down like a tidal wave. For some, all the above may be very genuine concerns. For others, they may just be unfounded worries. Nevertheless, the financial situation must be faced and dealt with. (See Chapter 3 for examples on how to weather this particular storm.)

The real challenge at the moment is not so much what you will do, but how to manage the panic. Often what you worry about never happens. The concern, however, can be paralyzing. You need to understand this process so you can eliminate the dread, accept what has happened, and be able to take appropriate action.

Keep in mind that how you act will affect how others hear the news. You need to get yourself as OK as possible before talking to others. This does not mean you put off telling the news. Instead, you need to be sure about what you are going to say and how you are going to say it. Get help from HR at work. Talk with a friend or co-worker to practice how you will deliver the news. Do what it takes to make yourself ready to face your family and friends.

Now it is time to do some reality checking. Examine your finances and be ready to make some reasonable decisions based on facts, not fright. Discuss all of the details with your spouse. Talk to the kids. If they are old enough they may not only be willing, but happy to help out. They may also be afraid. You need to listen to one another and to look for outside help. It may be a member of the clergy, the EAP counselor, a financial planner, close friend, next door neighbor or family member. You might also consider consulting with someone who lived through your same circumstances. If you are not acquainted with someone who had a similar experience, look for a support group that meets in a local church or synagogue that may offer some assistance. Your community college might have a discussion group, workshop, or counselor who can assist you at this time. Just reach out.

Scenario 1-2

Fear: Client Case
A 53 year old man worked for the same company for 26 years. After a buy-out he had been offered a transfer out of state. He turned it down because he did not want to leave his family, friends and networks. Within two weeks he had a job offer from an old friend and went right to work thinking everything he valued and his current standard of living would stay the same. There were problems on the new job and within two years he was

fired—by his best friend! Now he really was scared!

He was sure he would lose his house, car and the respect of his family. He was concerned about finding another job at his age. What now?

He went to see a career counselor and after about two hours of talking he could move beyond his crippling dread. He began to look at alternatives. Just hearing himself verbalize all the awful things he was thinking made him realize that most, if not all of his concerns, were either false or manageable.

After that sense of anxiety abates, another emotion may take hold and present its own trials.

Anger:

You are angry. If you do not feel that anger, you are probably suppressing it. It is natural and normal to feel anger and resentment. You will go through an experience similar to a grieving or mourning process. It begins with shock and anger, moves through denial, negotiation, and finally acceptance.

Even if you knew it was coming. Even if you hoped it would be you. Even if you hated your job. Even if you thought you were dead-ended and would have no future. Even if you thought it was best for the company. You will still be angry. When we think we are prepared for the death of a loved one or friend, when it actually happens, we still feel shocked and angry. It's OK. It's normal, predictable, and inescapable.

So what can you do with your anger? First, recognize it. You might want to blame your boss, CEO, HR manager, the messenger, or anyone else you feel is responsible. Staying angry keeps you stuck in place, so you can't move forward.

Assess the Present 17

Talk about it. Find someone who will listen. You do not necessarily need advice at this time, just ask for an ear. Saying all the things you are feeling is the beginning of dealing with matters in a healthy way. Find someone who will be able to hear you without trying to fix everything. This is called venting. Just like steam that builds up and needs to be released, you need to do the same.

You may feel like retreating and have some symptoms of depression. Consult a professional. Many companies offer Employee Assistance Programs that you can access after your separation. Use it. If not, consider talking with a mental health professional. It may not take more than a couple of sessions, but you may need help to successfully manage your crisis.

It is appropriate to be self-focused, willing to give yourself the support and time you need to cope with your loss. If you do not take care of yourself in the beginning, you will find it very hard to manage the task of the job search with energy, enthusiasm and success. Also, you need to be able to give your family support. You'll get stronger helping them.

Time should be long enough for you to dissipate the strong emotion of anger and the feelings of resentment, but not long enough to wallow. Self-pity is often the next step after anger, but it is very self-defeating. Poor YOU! You may feel like a victim on occasion, but do not allow that visitor to stay more than a moment. Open the door, look it in the face, shut the door and then carry on.

Scenario 1-3

Anger: Client Case
A friend called to say that he had been "canned." He had been employed by the hospital for 28 years.

They did not renew his contract. Instead, they awarded it to a younger physician. He was MAD! This had happened several weeks before, but he had been unable to tell any of his friends. Although it would be several months before the separation takes place, he was so angry he could hardly talk about it without raging and shouting. And he was depressed. He was seeing a therapist on a regular basis and was taking a mild antidepressant. When he calmed down he said he knew that it was coming because of the budget situation. New hires cost less. He had also been considering retiring from the administrative role anyway. But now the decision was out of his hands. He volunteered that he knew he would be OK financially, and the loss of the extra responsibility was not unwelcome, but, he was still incensed. He felt his loyalty had been dismissed. After all, 28 years of service is considerable.

His fury had been reduced to resentment after going through outrage, hostility, and indignation. As time passed, the intensity of his feelings subsided somewhat, especially when he acknowledged that he was considering the same route on his own. Talking it out with family and friends who encouraged him to welcome the retirement he would have chosen anyway, helped him get unstuck from his anger, so he could move on with his life.

So now, you can think about your situation without overwhelming anger and self-pity. Getting to this point may take a couple of weeks or just a day. It will vary for each person.

Assess the Present

Denial:

Denial can be tricky. Many separated employees who receive severance packages will avoid beginning the job search as long as the severance pay lasts. There are many reasons for doing this. Some feel that they have experienced such trauma that they need and deserve the time to recover. There is truth in needing recovery time, but to link it with severance pay will affect your ability to manage all of the details that will best serve your future interests. Severance pay may make denial worse, unless it is used only to help you manage the crisis, rather than remain stuck.

Those people who hold on to the "angry mode" may view income as something the corporation owes them and they are going to use it to take a vacation or travel. This option also has some merit, but make sure you are doing it for the right reason. Take some time off. You have been under stress and need some time to review the situation. Try to extract some learning from it in terms of your responses and expectations. Also, consider the reality of the business environment. These are all good meditation or reflection topics. But don't get trapped into letting severance pay become a way to avoid the reality of facing the inevitable need to take your next step toward reemployment or starting your own business.

Having said all that, what should you be doing if and while the severance pay is coming in? If you need it, take some time, but be reasonable. Consider using 10% of your time for recovery, relaxation and reflection. Take that time for yourself. Then it is time to face the reality of the future and take charge of how you are going to proceed. You have just been on the receiving end of someone else's decision. If you choose to, you may now make your own decisions. Determine how and where you want to be working in the future. Accept the fact that you are in charge. Only you can take the next steps.

Imagine yourself pushing through a barrier. That's a good way to describe moving through denial. It is real and often feels impenetrable. You do have the ability to push it aside. Get the help you need by using your resources. Listen to others who have dealt with rejection and redirection. Their stories will help you see the possibilities. This is a time to learn more about yourself.

Most likely, you are not facing this kind of a challenge for the first time. You have probably successfully dealt with obstacles and used your psychic strength to move forward. The skills you used to do this before are still yours to use now.

Remember to take care of yourself. Do what you must to get the help you need so you can take the next step. This is not the time to be a super-person. You have been helpful to others in the past, so give them the opportunity to return the favor. If you felt good because of your ability to help others, give your friends and family the same chance. You may find it hard to ask. After all, you have just been let down and may still be having feelings of inadequacy, which make it more difficult to generate a request. If it helps, promise yourself that you will help someone else in a similar situation. You may be absolutely sure that someone you know will have the same experience in the future, not as sure as taxes and death, but good enough to bet on!

Scenario 1-4

Denial: Client Case
A young man who spent 10 years in the Marines finally opted for civilian life, earned his B.S. in Marketing and took a job with a leading daily

newspaper in a large city. The paper had a history of more than 100 years, so he believed he had a good future. Two years into the job his entire department was eliminated. He was out of a job with six months severance pay. Six months seemed like plenty of time to find work. He would just take a few weeks to rest and catch up with some friends he had not seen because of his busy work schedule. The weeks turned into months and he found himself without work and with no income.

This situation is not uncommon. It is much more comfortable for all concerned to face the music and begin that job search before you find yourself borrowing money, or as he did, taking a low paying job with hourly wages just to pay the rent.

Negotiation:

Having managed the anger and moved beyond denial, the next logical step is negotiation. Some people will call their former boss or supervisor and try to negotiate for their former job suggesting lower pay, shorter hours, or adjusted workload. Anything to get the job back. They may call former coworkers and ask them to intercede for them with management. They create long lists of accomplishments and successes to back up their request. This approach is doomed. There are few if any examples of victory using this strategy.

Some try to bargain with fate. You can pray, send out 100 resumes, make 50 networking contacts, and hope that everything will work out. And, then it doesn't. Bargaining with fate is less profitable than trying to deal with fellow humans.

Keep in mind that this phase is normal and is generally more short-lived than the previous two. It is possible, however, to get caught in the cycle of thinking that hints you just might not have found the right formula. If you just keep revising the approach, you will be able to get that job back. You can see how this approach can push you back into denial and even back to square one with anger. This is the rut that you want to recognize and acknowledge. Move beyond this stage quickly. Think positively and take action. You just need to be careful to take the appropriate action.

Scenario 1-5

Negotiation: Client Case

A construction engineer was very active in his church and taught adult education classes. He believed that his Christian service had earned him some special merit with the Almighty. If he prayed hard enough then what he needed would be available. He forgot the adage that suggests we pray as if all is in the hands of God, but work as if all is in our hands. After many hours of praying, beseeching others to pray for him, and attending extra services, weeks went by with no results.

Can you guess what happened? Right back to anger and frustration. Do not pass go and do not collect $200. Is there anything wrong in what this gentleman did? Absolutely not! But it isn't good enough to generate a job offer. Perhaps his requests to others to pray may reach someone who can help him through networking, but the odds are slim that prayerful action will do much without worldly pro-action.

Acceptance:

The final phase of reaction to the news of dismissal is acceptance. You are ready to face reality. You are not the same person who started this journey. All the stages you have faced and moved through have altered you. You are stronger. Adversity has a way of offering that gift. You may even feel some satisfaction.

Life, we are told, is a series of lessons. The lessons are often difficult and challenging. Job loss will test your maturity, morality, relationships, reasoning ability, and emotional stability. With a little help from your family, friends, and professionals, you can look forward to a future that may be different from your original plan. Maybe this is not so bad after all and perhaps more satisfying.

Scenario 1-6

Acceptance: Client Case
- A health care administrator had been in her profession almost 20 years, working at the community hospital in the town where she was born and raised. She claimed she liked her work, enjoyed the stability of her lifestyle, and had no great career expectations, other than the status quo. However, things changed in the profession. She did not stay current with her management techniques, and finally, after many warnings that she did not heed, was fired.
- During her sessions with the career advisor she recalled a childhood dream to travel and work with children. This future had seemed too risky for her when she entered college, so she opted for a business major and a job in administration. Now she could re-examine that choice. She was single, had some severance pay and savings,

and could return to school to take some education courses and then possibly join the Peace Corps. Maybe after all these years of doing something she liked, she could now do something she loved!

The real world is tough. It is a hard teacher and task-master. Still, you have made it this far and are now ready to assess yourself, your situation, your environment, and ready to take some positive action.

❧ ❧ ❧

Chapter Two

> **STRENGTHEN SELF AWARENESS**
>
> ❧❧❧
>
> **Course of Action Number 2**

Introduction

Chapter 2 will help you to identify and to evaluate alternatives. You need to be fully aware of your emotions, dreams and real barriers. This is a "taking stock" opportunity for you. You will do some reflection on your history and learn how to use your natural gifts and talents to discover the kind of work you really want.

❧ ❧ ❧

Don't Shoot the Messenger

Your employment is over. You have cleaned out your desk or locker, turned in your keys and equipment. You have collected all of the details about your benefits, your severance pay, and your unemployment compensation. Any relevant material you need to terminate your relationship with your former employer was submitted. Now, it really is over.

You have accepted the truth of the situation. You know that you have to move forward, but you may still feel some sense of unfinished business. There may still be nightmares about how the message was delivered to you. Perhaps you still have moments of returning rage when you think about your treatment. Let's take a minute to look at this and see what, if anything, might be helpful to you.

Begin with your feelings. They are real and quite frankly, predictable. Recognize that they will surface at times you might least expect them to occur. If you have read the previous chapter and really worked your way through the steps of reaction, you may be somewhat surprised to have these recurring emotions. Not to worry. But also, not to dwell. This is time for action and you will have lots of practice moving through the feelings. Just recognize that it will happen. Do not give yourself grief about the recurrence. Acknowledge it and keep on keeping on.

Don't forget your support team during these occurrences. Ask for help. Talk about it to relieve the tension. You are not looking for advice, just an ear.

But what about your former employer? Surely, you have some real friends and colleagues who remained with the firm. Should you just write them all off because of their association with the company that let you go, or should you reach out for support? Don't assume that they will be unwilling to assist you on your search. Make some overtures to discover what kinds of assistance might be available. And don't shoot the messenger! It may be a bit like shooting yourself in the foot!

Problems, Challenges, and Opportunities

Keep in mind that some of your former coworkers may be feeling guilty because they survived the cutback. Be sensitive when you contact them and set up an appointment to meet. You can be sure that they will want to help but may feel uncomfortable. Do your best to assure them that you are not vengeful and that you recognize the reasons for the actions taken. You are seeking their help to move forward, not to get revenge or whine!

These colleagues may be very helpful in identifying new employment opportunities in other settings. They may also want to hear from you to be sure that you are doing OK. They could be on the next reduction list and seeing you do well will be supportive to them. So, even though you are the one on the outside looking in, the inside may not feel any more secure than your environment.

Scenario 2-1

Winds of Change: Client Case

A long time employee with a Fortune 100 company was let go with a nice severance package. He was a manager, not an executive. His package was respectable, but would not sustain him until retirement age. At 50 years of age, he still wanted to work. He already met and worked with the outplacement firm that the company had hired to help those let go. What was evident from the self-assessment and counseling he received was that he did not want to return to the same work he just left. He did it for years and was ready for a more flexible schedule and less stress and pressure.

Why couldn't he work with the outplacement firm helping others, like himself, who had been dismissed? He had completed lots of training for the company, therefore he was comfortable facilitating workshops. Having gone through the outplacement process himself, he believed he could be empathetic and show others how to make decisions and how to take advantage of future options. Wasn't he doing that right now?

The outplacement manager offered him the opportunity to go through their train-the-trainer program and then, to give the job a try. He loved the interaction and working with people to develop and go after new goals. His initial workshop trainees returned very positive evaluations. A new career was launched. The very trend that pushed him out of work provided an opportunity for new professional challenges and rewards.

He works on contracts for the outplacement company and in between assignments he fishes, travels and spends time with his grandchildren. Everyone was a winner in this scenario.

❧ ❧ ❧

Alternative Courses of Action

In spite of the promise of success, there are still some very real problems that must be addressed before success becomes a reality. The first is to take stock of what you have to offer a new employer, or what you might need to do to start your own business.

Strengthen Self Awareness

One of the first things you want to be clear about is your passion. What are you doing when you feel most effective, most competent and most fulfilled? What will get you up early in the morning or keep you out of bed until late at night? Think about the kind of activities that are fulfilling to you.

No matter which road you ultimately take, you need some data upon which to make your decision. How do you gather that and where do you go to make that happen?

There are several routes available to you, depending on where you live and what the community has to offer. But, the first step is self-assessment. Find out what skills and abilities you want to use in the future. Be clear about what your favorite accomplishments are so you can repeat them. Get some clarity on the best environment for your best work. Do you know what your values are? You may not have asked yourself many of these questions for years, if at all. So you are on a quest to discover your best self and find the best way to describe that best self to others. That description will open doors for you to explore so you can choose among alternatives for the best placement.

How, you might ask, am I going to get all this information about myself? Let's begin by exploring what is available to you through your community. Community colleges, local school systems, and state and local agencies often have workshops and professional counselors to assist workers who have lost their jobs. These services are accessible and often are free or offered at a very low cost. Some local libraries have career advisors on site a few hours a week to provide information, support, and direction. What you should be asking for at this point are self-assessment tools and exercises that will provide feedback so that you can tailor your resume to the type of work you want to do. Also, you may want to examine whether or not self-employment is an option.

Your company may offer free workshops as part of your outplacement process; take advantage of them. Our experience with these programs indicates very few eligible people sign up and take these workshops. Reasons often given have to do with the anger and denial about the job loss. These offerings are usually scheduled right after the layoff and perhaps some people are not feeling ready. It seems a shame to let such a rich resource go unused. Don't you be caught in that bind!

Scenario 2-2

The Turn On: Client Case

A young man who really hated his job and believed he was going to be fired for his poor performance, said that the only thing he really loved doing was surfing. On the surface, that does not sound like an indication of work ambitions. What he said he loved most about it was the research he did before he traveled to the surfing spot. He investigated tides, wave patterns, shorelines, and wind. When asked if he really enjoyed the ride he said what really excited him was when all the work he had done came together and he knew the ride would be a good one. It wasn't the wave riding as much as gathering all the data to insure the successful ride. As part of his job he conducted research but was no longer a part of the final project. The aspect of seeing it all come together was missing.

So he returned to his job and negotiated for that part of the process and once again was happy in his job and performing well.

Strengthen Self Awareness

Knowing what really turns you on, whether you identify it as work or play, is a critical piece of information about yourself. It can go a long way to helping you choose your next job and doing what you love.

You also need to be able to clearly state what your best skills are. Ask some friends or family members what they think you do best. Ask colleagues or former work associates. You will collect a long list of what OTHERS see you doing well. Often this list helps you to get a better picture of the real you. Look for patterns in their answers. Look for repetition of skills. Look for what excites you when they talk about it.

Scenario 2-3

Listen Up: Client Case

An office worker who was unhappy in her task-oriented job carried out such a skills assessment assignment. To her surprise she found that her coworkers and family repeatedly talked about what a good listener she was. They said she would make a great counselor.

Although she had never considered returning to school after earning her Bachelor's degree, the idea of becoming a professional counselor was truly appealing. She realized that she always had time to help coworkers and friends solve problems. She loved doing it! It had seemed so easy and natural that she never felt like it was work. Imagine getting paid to do what you do well naturally!

So she stayed at her job, enrolled in a graduate program and finally landed a job as an academic advisor at a community college.

Another way to get at the same information is to make a list of your accomplishments. These are things you have done and enjoyed doing. These successes may have been recognized by others. Begin with your youth. List awards, honors or trophies you won in school doing the things you liked. Add those things you have done at work that have been recognized. Finally, complete your list with those things you have done as a volunteer that have earned you recognition or even just a feeling of accomplishment.

Now, review that list. Think about what skills you used to do those things. Write it down. These skills represent what you do when you are successful and happy. If you get to do what you love and are good at it, you will succeed. History just proved that to you with your list.

Now, what among those activities would you like to repeat? What would you like to create again in your life? Don't think about what kind of a job you will need at this time. Just think about the activities.

Scenario 2-4

Act One: Client Case
A woman listed all the plays and shows she used to create during her summer vacations in her earlier days. She put on some elaborate productions. In high school and college, she always volunteered to help with plays and everyone thought she did a great job. She had never considered how this experience could translate to work. Today she manages all the conferences and seminars her financial management company offers to customers. She finds the right location, arranges speakers, plans the food and social activities and makes sure all the materials are on hand. Quite a production! Not in the theatre, but using all the

same skills, she loves her work. Incidentally, she still works as a volunteer in community theatre.

Another piece of personal information that is vital to this assessment is to identify your special knowledge. Often there are things that you have learned, simply because of your interest in a particular subject. This may be knowledge that you can use in paid work.

What kinds of books do you read? What kinds of movies do you choose to watch? What are your hobbies? What kinds of workshops have you chosen to attend?

The answers to these questions are strong clues to the kind of knowledge you have accumulated over the years that can help you take a new direction or put a new spin on an old one.

When you have listed all these facts, review the list for patterns. Is your interest history, cooking, horticulture, or mechanics? Have you taken craft workshops? Do you love mysteries?

Scenario 2-5

Revelations: Client Case

A mystery book lover realized that she only read those books so she could figure out what was happening before the writer revealed it. She loved guessing the outcome before it was uncovered. Previously, she had been working in management for years and had always wanted to be more involved in planning, but felt unqualified. After recognizing her ability to read a scenario, look for clues, and figure out the best way to solve a problem, she began to volunteer for task forces at work. No longer with that employer, she now works as a consultant for similar firms. Her ability to interview employees, read documentation about procedures, and to discover the source of problems is uncanny. She can hardly believe that her love for Nancy Drew mysteries as a child, which she continued to support throughout her adult reading life, actually reflected her best knowledge. She learned much about talking to people to get information, looking at written material, following a process and then "solving the mystery." What fun!

What you learn about during your lifetime through self-assessment provides you with a special knowledge. It can give you clues about what to do next. You are considering important information about yourself that you had not even been aware of in the past.

Scenario 2-6

Into The Woods: Client Case

A gentleman who was taking early retirement from a large utility company was in his early fifties. He was ready to leave the work he had done for 30 years, but was too full of energy to play golf for the next 30 years. He talked about his hobby of woodworking. During his lifetime, he had learned how to work with different woods. He knew all about where different trees were grown, which were best for different kinds of furniture and carpentry tasks, all about the aging of woods and how that should affect the way it is used in building. He was truly an expert in the field. He had never taken a course or workshop but had read everything he could get his hands on. Each time he worked with a new wood or a new project, he not only read about it, but he also developed a network of professionals in the field whom he consulted for help.

What he recognized during a discussion of this lifelong passion was the research skills he used, as well as his talent for woodworking. He decided to put together a business plan to open his own company doing custom work. In truth, he already had a list of satisfied customers, people he had worked for in the past for the cost of materials only. These friends and neighbors had often suggested that he go into business for himself but he was unwilling to give up all the benefits of the utility company job. That was no longer an issue.

He also decided to contact the local high school and community college to see if there were any teaching opportunities. His knowledge of woods as well as his skill would make him an excellent instructor. In the past he often worked with neighborhood kids who came to his home workshop for advice.

If all of the options work out, our retiree is going to be as busy as he was when employed full-time. He will make money doing what he has loved all his life. Using his natural gift and talents, he will be fulfilled as well as financially rewarded. Post-retirement now appears as an exciting late life challenge instead of a boring proposition.

Another important aspect of self-assessment is values clarification. Values define our lives and provide meaning. They drive our decisions. Many people do not take time during their busy lives to examine their values and look at what is truly important. At a time of job loss or career change, it is an ideal task to insure that your decision for the next step really creates a lifestyle in keeping with your best wishes. Decisions made without this deliberation can lead to dissatisfaction. Often the individual is not aware why the dissatisfaction occurs. Looking at values can help you to choose wisely and well.

Values represent worth or desirability. Values reflect a vital and integral part of you. Values are deeply held. When we argue with loved ones and cannot seem to come to agreement, the odds are that you differ in your values. No amount of logic or analysis will persuade another against values.

What is a value? How do you define and describe them? You can find lists of them in many career redirection books. Here is one list for you to consider:

Table 2-1

VALUE SYSTEMS

Accomplishment	Expertise	Pleasure
Acknowledgment	Family	Recognition
Autonomy	Friendship	Spirituality
Challenge	Honesty	Variety
Cooperation	Intimacy	Wealth
Creativity	Leisure	

The task is to identify which of these are important to you and then to decide which two or three are most important. Prioritizing these values leads to better self-understanding and decision making.

Values are related to needs. What you value is what you need in your life to feel satisfied. When we make decisions or have experiences that meet our stated and unstated needs, we evaluate those decisions and experiences as valuable.

Strengthen Self Awareness

Scenario 2-7

Self-Directed: Client Case

A middle-aged woman was job hunting. Her previous position had been eliminated in a reorganization, so she was unemployed. During the two interviews she had landed, she made it a point to ask about the management style of the person she would report to, if hired. Her questions indicated her high value for autonomy. She always asked if the boss preferred to assign a task and then give the employee freedom to carry it out. She wanted to find out if the boss would prefer to work with or oversee the work of the employee. Her past experience had made it clear that she strongly prefers to run with the job, asking for help only when needed. She knew she was most effective working that way. In a situation where there was lots of supervision, she felt stressed, anxious, and downright irritable.

When she met with the V.P. for Human Resources about the job being offered, he detailed how busy he was and how he needed someone who could take the reins and run. The need was music to her ears. She then gave examples of how she had done that in past jobs and been successful. She not only got the job, she loved it and her boss thought she was terrific.

Using your knowledge of your highly held values in interviewing can allow you to make a good choice for a good match.

Your values often come through in your language and the stories you tell about yourself in your interviews and resume. Be sure you are picking stories that best reflect what you esteem most significantly.

Scenario 2-8

The Mismatch: Client Case

During a job interview, an applicant spent lots of time describing how hard he worked, telling lengthy stories about his very high energy levels, and accomplishments in the past. He further emphasized his willingness to work overtime (which was clearly stated as important by the recruiter). He landed the job.

This young man had recently married and joined a softball team. The necessity to work evenings and weekends was no longer attractive to him. He now had to decide if the job was worth giving up his leisure time, which was always important to him. Until he married, it never really was a problem, even with working overtime.

So our young man began to react negatively to overtime requests. He would not accept some assignments, he left early on some occasions, and his job performance began to slip.

Sometimes a life change, like marriage or the birth of a child, can create a different situation. If we have not examined our values, we may not understand our deep dissatisfaction when that value can no longer be met. By the end of the probation period, it was clear that it was not working and the young man found himself looking for another job.

After discussing the situation with his spouse he realized the problem and on future interviews was clear about how much overtime he was willing to take. The next job, which did not pay as much, worked out fine. Wealth was not a high value for this young family, but time together was.

Dealing With It

In order to deal effectively with the issues of seeking new employment, take the time to examine your skills, knowledge and values. Being clear about what is important to you makes the job search more rewarding. Most workers will move from job to job and perhaps career to career several times during their work life. Indeed, it is possible for you to identify the kinds of work situations that meet your needs as well as the employers. This effort will increase your chances of success and happiness.

Chapter Three

UTILIZE FINANCIAL TOOLS

❧❧❧

Course of Action Number 3

Introduction

Let's shift gears and move into the technical side of the layoff equation. Fasten your seatbelts for a run through some statistics.

❧ ❧ ❧

The Long-Range Forecast

Prevailing stormy winds of change. Partly bad news, but lots of good news. The storm is charged with a cold blast of inevitable change. You may find security with solid and timely knowledge coupled with adaptability to the forthcoming new job environment.

Unfortunately, mass layoffs will continue. Let's take a look at some of the facts and we will find that there is some basis for optimism. For example, the U.S.

Department of Labor reported that 45% of employers reporting a layoff in the second quarter of 2001 indicated that they anticipated a recall of some type. Downsized employees who worked for their employer for more than three years were classified as long-tenured workers. A study was conducted of long-tenured workers who were displaced between January 1997 and December 1999. This group was comprised of 3.3 million people. It was learned that 74% of this group was re-employed when surveyed in February 2000. The reemployment rate was the highest for workers in the age group of 20 to 54.

Companies reported plant closings or company relocations as the main reasons for the layoff of the long-tenured workers. Persons working in manufacturing were the largest group of those downsized and were the least likely to be re-employed. In recent periods, the high-paying manufacturing jobs have accounted for about 41% of all layoffs. However, about one-fourth of these workers were later re-employed in a similar job. Some workers in this category reported earnings losses of 20% or more, but the majority, 58% of this group, reported earnings the same or greater than those of their former job.

The Department of Labor conducted a study that reports the reasons offered by employers for extended mass layoffs. These findings appear in Table 3-1.

Table 3-1

REASONS FOR EXTENDED MASS LAYOFFS (2001)

In order of number of workers impacted

1. Seasonal Work
2. Slack Work
3. Contract Completed
4. Reorganization
5. Financial Difficulty
6. Bankruptcy
7. *"Not Reported"
8. *"Other"
9. Ownership Change
10. Contract Cancelled
11. Import Competition
12. Overseas Relocation
13. Weather-related
14. Domestic Relocation
15. Product Line Dropped
16. Energy Related
17. Plant or Machine Repair
18. Automation
19. Material Shortage
20. Model Changeover

*It is unclear where these classifications might be reallocated without further study.

Given this list as a reference, you can match some of the present conditions in your organization with causes for layoffs. If several of these 20 listed reasons are in play, it may be a solid indicator of forthcoming layoffs.

The predictions that follow are based on research data compiled by the U.S. Bureau of Labor Statistics relating to the period of 1998 to 2008. The 10-year forecast expects the size of the workforce to grow by 14%. The age group of 45 to 64 will grow faster than any other age group because of the aging of the baby-boom generation. The age group of 25 to 34 years will decline by about 2.7 million workers because of a decline in the birth rate during the late 1960s and early 1970s. The service producing industries will provide almost all of the job growth. More specifically, health services, business services, social services, engineering, and management are forecast to provide about one half of all new jobs. Precision production, craft, machine repair, operators, fabricators and laborer jobs will grow very slowly because of technological innovation.

Here again, we are reminded of an external environmental condition over which we have no control.

The top ten occupations with the fastest employment growth predictions are given in Table 3-2. The top ten occupations with the largest expected job growth are listed in Table 3-3.

Table 3-2
FASTEST JOB GROWTH PROSPECTS TO YEAR 2008
by Job Title

1. Computer Engineers
2. Computer Support Specialists
3. Systems Analysts
4. Database Administrators
5. Desktop Publishing Specialists
6. Paralegals and Legal Assistants
7. Personal and Home Care Aides
8. Medical Assistants
9. Social and Human Service Assistants
10. Physician Assistants

Table 3-3
LARGEST JOB GROWTH PROSPECTS TO YEAR 2008
by Job Title

1. Systems Analysts
2. Retail Salespersons
3. Cashiers
4. General Managers and Top Executives
5. Truck Drivers (Light and Heavy)
6. Office Clerks
7. Registered Nurses
8. Computer Support Specialists
9. Personal Care and Home Health Aides
10. Teacher Assistants

Studies to year 2008 indicate that business services, health care, social services, engineering and management services will account for about 50% of job growth. Temporary jobs through "Temp Agencies" are expected to generate many jobs. These jobs help the individual in the short run, but typically have lower wages, are very unstable, and provide few benefits.

Manufacturing organizations are expected to continue a trend of decline. Manufacturing jobs accounted for 13% of employment in 1998, and the number is expected to decrease to about 12% by 2008.

Jobs that require the most education will be the fastest growing and also the highest paying. Conversely, jobs that require the least education will provide many openings, but will be the lowest paying.

🐸 🐸 🐸

Circumstances

After considering the job market forecast, we may more realistically deal with the many different job and economic life stage situations on the horizon. Some are brief visits and others are long term. For example, you may have been downsized and had to deal with the difficulties of being unemployed for a short period of time or, unfortunately, a longer term. Or you may be offered an early retirement incentive and be able to live quite comfortably within your current lifestyle. Or you may have accrued enough personal wealth to not worry about returning to the workplace after a job loss. If you are very fortunate, you may have an avocation that is likely to become a successful vocation. Although there are varied economic circumstances, we will focus on a typical real world situation where one chooses to (or must) return to the job market.

Scenario 3-1

Sea of Debt: Client Case
A middle-aged man received an unexpected layoff notice on Friday, effective that day. He was told that he would be given one month's pay as a severance benefit. He was angry, embarrassed, and deeply hurt. His reaction was to laugh it off and

tell others that he would pick up another job with higher pay next week. He did not accept the reality of unemployment and continued to live "normally" without regard to depletion of his savings. After all, from his frame of reference, it was a very poor move on the part of the company to lay him off and "they" will pay for their mistake.

He was not able to find a job in the next month, nor the next ten months. He was caught in a spiral of decline where one bad situation led to another. His assets were depleted and his self-esteem had bottomed out. He allowed his ego to interfere with his pragmatism.

ફ્રા ફ્રા ફ્રા

Damage Control

It is essential that you stabilize your position before the torrents of circumstance erupt into economic shredders. Your assets must be identified before they can be protected and efficiently employed. We will describe two categories of assets, (1) tangible, those that are economic and (2) "personal" intangible, those that are part of a family or collegian support system. It is important to quickly recognize the reality of your situation. Ego involvement with self-pride or self-regard resulting in denial of your status, may negatively interact with the process of recovery. Unemployment means that you are not generating any revenue from your services. Non-acceptance of this fact, because of ego involvement or any other reason, will result in a loss of precious time and may lead to rapid depletion of resources.

Of course, there are occasions where volunteer or other non-compensatory jobs are available. This may be a short-term option for networking purposes, but is unlikely to provide for any immediate financial needs.

How Will I Manage

Tangible Assets:
As the name implies, tangible assets are those with measurable qualities. Examples of tangible assets are: cash from savings, severance pay, loan values from insurance policies, automobiles, residence, recreational vehicles, personal property, and financial assistance from various governmental agencies.

"Personal" Intangible Assets:
Personal intangible assets are those that have significant value, but are difficult to quantify. We may say that these assets comprise a personal support system. Intangible assets may be derived from family members and friends who offer such needed support as encouragement, job leads, baby-sitting assistance, social interaction, spiritual reinforcement, or maybe just a shoulder to cry on. As important as these assets are, they do not fit into a quantifiable analysis, and therefore will not appear on an economic balance sheet. However, if there is such a thing as an emotional balance sheet the personal intangible assets certainly would be an integral part.

Utilize Financial Tools 49

Liabilities:

Simply stated, liabilities are amounts that are owed. Some examples of liabilities are mortgages, auto loans, credit card balances, insurance payments due, and personal loans.

It is a good idea to construct a personal balance sheet to have a clear vision of your current financial resources. The balance sheet equation is: net worth is equal to the sum of assets minus liabilities. A sample balance sheet is shown on page 50.

The balance sheet provides a snapshot of your financial position at a given point in time. It is advisable to update your balance sheet at least once a year. This financial statement illustrates the current status of your economic life.

Revenue and Disbursements:

Let's look at the revenue side of personal finance. Revenues are dollars that are brought in and placed into the hopper to sustain a lifestyle and possibly to accrue wealth. In order to keep our example simple, we will consider the revenue amounts as after tax dollars. Revenue includes such items as; wages, interest payments received, rent received, unemployment benefits, government subsidies such as tuition reimbursement, and disability insurance receipts. Disbursements are payments made. These payments include expenses and liabilities. Examples of disbursements are payments for mortgages, taxes, automobiles, utilities, and insurance. Revenue and disbursements should be conservatively forecasted. You should estimate revenue on the low side and disbursements on the high side.

BALANCE SHEET
of
I. M. Down
As of April 30, 200x

Tangible Assets
    Cash on Hand $1,750
    Cash in bank 13,750

    Real Estate
        Residence 197,000
        Summer cottage 95,000
        Building lot 27,000

    Automobiles
        200x Nissan Altima 17,000
        200x Ford Bronco 16,500

    Recreational Vehicle ....
        199x Motor Home 13,500

    Retirement Accounts
        ABC Corp. (vested) 83,000
        IRA 11,000
        SRA 6,500
    Personal Property 3,000
Total Tangible Assets **$485,000**

Liabilities
    Mortgage Payable Residence .... $ 73,000
    Automobile loans 4,200
    Credit Card Balances 1,800
    Insurance Premium due 900
Total Liabilities **$79,900**

Net Worth (Assets minus Liabilities) ***$405,100***
Total Liabilities and Net Worth $485,000

Utilize Financial Tools

Cash Budget:

The cash budget is a document that is easy to prepare and it offers the closest link to reality of any financial plan. A cash budget should be conservative and used as part of a fluid planning process and not just considered a static document that will be written then ignored. Two examples of cash budgets are given. (1) *The Way It Is With Unemployment*, and (2) *The Way It Must Be (Bridging The Gap)*. The cash budget may be written with a pencil and paper approach or with any computer spreadsheet program.

The budget that follows (page 52), reflects the status of unemployment by one spouse (salary 1).

The revised budget that follows (page 53), presents a much different picture. Since revenues do not match expenses and liabilities (a cash shortage) budget revisions must be made. Clearly, without resources to add to the inflow of cash (without incurring additional debt) a major problem is right around the corner.

Difficult choices and actions may have to be made in order to protect the major assests. This is the point where the ego kicks into high gear and interferes with the problem solving process.

After much thought and perhaps extensive soul searching, I. Will Winn has made some tough choices and established a new budget that will serve as a transition to the next step. Note that unemployment benefits were not included as a revenue source. This was left out to illustrate an ultraconservative approach to the cash budget. If unemployment is expected to be long-term, then net unemployment benefits should be added to revenues.

I. Will Winn
CASH BUDGET
The Way It Is With Unemployment

Each Month - April through October

Revenue Net—After Tax	Monthly	Totals
Salary 1	$ 0	$ 0
Salary 2	4,000	28,000
Interest Income	150	1,050
Other Sources of Funds		
Total Revenue	$ 4,150	$ 29,050
Disbursements		
Mortgage	900	6,300
Automobile Loan	240	1,680
Automobile Expense	125	875
Groceries	650	4,550
Utilities	540	3,780
Clothing	275	1,925
Home Furnishings	200	1,400
Home Improvements	400	2,800
Insurance—Life	200	1,400
Insurance—Other	200	1,400
Tuition	1,000	7,000
Entertainment	550	3,850
Credit Cards	100	700
Memberships	40	280
Publications	35	245
Donations	200	1,400
Other	250	1,750
Total Disbursements	$ 5,905	$ 41,335
Excess or (Shortage)	($ 1,755)	($12,285)

I. Will Winn
CASH BUDGET
The Way It Must Be
(Bridging The Gap)

Each Month - April through October

Revenue Net—After Tax	Monthly	Totals
Salary 1	$ 0	$ 0
Salary 2	4,000	28,000
Interest Income	150	1,050
Other Sources of Funds		
Total Revenue	$ 4,150	$ 29,050
Disbursements		
Mortgage	450	3,150
Automobile Loan	120	840
Automobile Expense	125	875
Groceries	650	4,550
Utilities	540	3,780
Clothing	275	1,925
Home Furnishings	100	700
Home Improvements	200	1,400
Insurance—Life	200	1,400
Insurance—Other	200	1,400
Tuition	0	0
Entertainment	280	1,960
Credit Cards	100	700
Memberships	40	280
Publications	35	245
Donations	100	700
Other	250	1,750
Total Disbursements	$ 3,665	$ 25,655
Excess or (Shortage)	$ 485	$ 3,395

Let's consider some of the options that were explored and found to be invaluable for Mr. Winn. He contacted his bank and was able to negotiate one-half payment on his mortgage for the next 12 months, which significantly reduces the amount of cash required for his monthly budget. He received permission to do the same with his automobile loan, and thereby further reduced his monthly cash outlay. Of course, any deferral in paying liabilities will result in additional interest charges, but given the choice of that or default on payments, perhaps the extra interest is not the worst choice.

Other budget line items were worked on and reduced. The line items of home furnishings and home improvements were cut in half and entertainment was likewise reduced. Donations may have to be trimmed, but remember that you must first be positioned to help yourself and your family through difficult times before you have any obligation to help others. Monthly accruals for tuition payments are eliminated because Mr. Winn was able to secure a Stafford student loan in his daughter's name and it does not have to be repaid until after she graduates. Further, there are many work/study programs at colleges, that will enable the student to soften the economic burden of tuition. It is not only unreasonable to try and cover all costs by yourself, but it can be downright hazardous to your health. All other line items were left intact. Now all expenses and liabilities may be paid in a timely fashion. Although the revenue section that is labeled, "other source of funds" was not changed, there are possibilities for additions to this section. For example, unemployment insurance benefits, drawing from savings accounts, borrowing the cash value of life insurance policies, selling personal property and liquidating stock may be potential sources of funding.

Beyond unemployment insurance, there are government sponsored programs that offer support for persons who have been affected by layoffs as a result of such major national changes as the North American Free Trade Agreement (NAFTA). Such programs provide financial assistance, college tuition, and other benefits.

Other help in balancing the budget may come from credit counselors. Some of the services they provide are credit and debt consolidation, individual and family budget preparation, credit report review and analysis, creditor negotiations and settlements, and attorney referrals. In many cases, bankers are willing to be very cooperative with mortgagors in an attempt to minimize defaults and subsequent costly foreclosures. Remember that although economic troubles are of concern they are not indicative of the end of the world. If all else fails there are bankruptcy laws designed to help the individual out of impossible situations; just because you lose your job doesn't mean that you have to lose everything else. Fortunately, we do not have debtors' prisons to worry about.

🙰 🙰 🙰

Interim Business

Consider starting a low investment, small business while conducting a job search. If the business turns out to be successful then you may want to continue with it. If success is not the outcome (or forecasted outcome) at least some of the expenses may result in a relief of part of your tax burden. Perhaps the most valuable benefit of starting a small business is the activity itself and a feeling of accomplishment. Also, it will provide documented evidence that you were employed during your search period. In other words, you will not have time gaps of inactivity to explain to prospective employers.

Sometimes financial gymnastics are necessary to protect your prime assets (such as your residence and automobiles) and will buy time to conduct a job search, which hopefully, will enable a return to an economic steady state. Obviously, there is a trade off when assets are liquidated and the cash is re-deployed or when the interest clock ticks for an extended period of time. Every situation is different, but approaching the problem in a systematic manner will contribute to more intelligent decisions and actions.

Implementation Plan:

An implementation plan is the lifeblood of a problem solution. This is the action plan. Concurrent with the preparation of your balance sheet and budget revisions other important activities should be underway. Urgent matters of job search planning and networking are discussed in Chapter 4. You must get going with financial and job search plans, avoid counterproductive ego involvement, keep the faith, and work the plan. Remember activism replaces anger and action replaces fear.

Moving On

Recognize the reality of the situation, get rid of denial (it will impede your progress), explore options, network, and prepare realistic financial statements. Remember you are not alone in your quest to get back on track and time is a non-renewable resource, so don't waste it; use it efficiently during your pursuits.

Scenario 3-2

A New Adventure: Client Case
- A man worked for an electronics firm for almost 10 years. He was laid off this past May because of contracted jobs being assigned to another plant in Mexico. Since his company lost jobs to a NAFTA (North American Free Trade Agreement) member country, displaced employees were granted special privileges for unemployment insurance.
- Under the special terms, discharged employees may collect unemployment for up to two years as long as they attend school or receive some type of approved occupational retraining. The company's government subsidized program allows the maximum unemployment benefit for two years, free tuition, books, and supplies to pursue a career oriented field of study at a local community college.
- The future for this now unemployed man, at 54 years old, lacking in education, and having a spotty work history, didn't look too promising. He decided to try the community college. He received advice and guidance from academic and career counselors and he agreed with them, that computer literacy should be foremost on his agen-

da. He enjoys problem solving, and is intrigued with the world of computers so he chose the curriculum of Business Programming and Systems. He found a fulfilling adventure in paving his new career path and it turned out to be a very profitable choice for him.

Scenario 3-3

A Helping Hand: Client Case

With no warning and an escorted trip from the desk to the parking lot, the investment counselor was advised that he lost his job. This man had many years of success in his field. He was recruited by the firm with promises of high commissions. Over time, impossible sales goals were set by his manager which eventually led to dismissal. So after a good employment history as a professional who had also volunteered countless hours to the community, this man was unemployed and distraught.

For a couple of weeks, he was immobilized. His friends would call to ask how much golf he was playing. But he was too dismayed to do much except hang out at the house. He had gone through self-reflection and knew that this was a temporary set back, but was not able to actively pursue new employment. The last job did not pay all that well in the end, so there were financial problems to consider.

Although successful up to the last job in the finance field, he had always wanted to work for an organization that really helped people in need. Many of his volunteer hours were spent working for institutions like United Way. He had effectively raised funds for non-profits and worked on community development issues. He saw himself as a competent team manager and loved to plan and organize. He worked effectively with other volunteers, and honed his skills in motivation and empowerment.

After discussing these assets and interests with a career counselor, he finally admitted that he had dreamed of running a not-for-profit organization but was concerned that the pay would not be adequate for his family needs. He had even been approached in the past about such jobs. He knew of two openings that he could now consider. He kept informed about these employment opportunities although he thought he could not afford to take such a job.

When he explored the salary and benefits, he discovered that the difference was not as great as he had assumed. Within one week he had interviewed, accepted an offer and started work. Two weeks later he was networking with other professionals in the community to enhance the work of his new job. And he enjoyed the fact that his talents and skills were supporting people in need.

Sudden dismissal in this case was a fortuitous opportunity for meaningful re-employment when there were several job openings. Being fired can sometimes present possibilities for the kind of work dreamed of but not pursued because of fear of rocking the boat. It is hard to leave a good job willingly to take another that pays less and has less prestige. But when all the risks and advantages are weighed, doing what you love is a good choice. The family will not be compromised and you get to use your talents and skills in service that meets your ideals of the dream job. It is great to get up in the morning and love the idea of going to work. It is even better if the work feels like play. When you are doing what you love, it does not always feel like work.

There are always articles in newspapers and magazines about successful people. Read them. They often speak to the beauty of following your heart, doing what you passionately love, making use of your talents and favorite skills. Your heart will sing! Those who live with and work with you will find you a more effective and competent individual. It is only scary until you do it. Use the experience of others as recorded in books and periodicals. Look for those stories. It is not always about movie stars and sports greats. Average (whatever that means) persons, often consider themselves average until they hook up with their passion. After doing work they love, they claim happiness, satisfaction and success. You only have one life to live. There is no dress rehearsal. So using your talents in service to others can bring you the best of all rewards. You are happy and fulfilled and the people you serve are all the better for your being there. You can make a difference if you choose. It takes courage. This action is much better than giving in to fear and then losing the chance for happiness in work.

ða ða ða

Something to Think About

Difficulty is a severe instructor, set over us by the supreme ordinance of a parental guardian and legislator, who knows us better than we know ourselves; and He loves us better too. He that wrestles with us strengthens our nerves, and sharpens our skill. Our antagonist is our helper. This amica-

ble conflict with difficulty obliges us to an intimate acquaintance with our object, and compels us to consider it in all its relations.
                                                            Burke

Chapter Four

HIGHLIGHT YOUR MANY VALUES

Course of Action Number 4

Introduction

This chapter will provide the methods to help you assess your personal and professional background in a structured format in the context of "marketing principles" for your job market portfolio. By using practices borrowed from the business world you will be better prepared to move onward from a dreadful situation to a calculated and clear course of action.

The Marketing Mix

There are four "P's" that comprise the marketing mix: product; promotion; place; and price. Business definitions of the four "P's" follow. A product is a good or service designed to satisfy a need or a want that is offered to a market for consumption. Products or services may include organizations, ideas, and persons. Promotion includes personal selling, advertising, goal advancement, and public relations. Place is the location where the product or service is available. Price is the dollar amount and/or other values that consumers pay for a product or service.

ès ès ès

You as the Product

It is important to recognize that you are a commodity in the workplace and that you must address this fact in a straightforward unabashed manner. If you conduct a "product" self-analysis you may be pleasantly surprised to learn how much you really have to offer. Refer to the checklist of "Product Self-analysis" for points to consider when defining yourself as a product. Keep in mind that during the interview process you may be asked questions relating to any or all of the "product" issues. For example, "How do you handle conflict on the job?" This is addressed later in the chapter.

Table 4-1
"PRODUCT" SELF-ANALYSIS

Education	Physical Limitations
Experience	Interpersonal Skills
Availability	Appearance
Reliability	Special Skills

Education:

Analysis of your education should include all appropriate experiences in a formal setting, such as college course work, on-the-job training, seminars attended, and other non-traditional learning experiences that you may have accumulated over the years. It is a good idea to keep your resume current, and in particular, to add all of the relevant details specifying recent educational accomplishments.

Experience:

Generally, work experience includes a myriad of job tasks, many major and some nominal. Further, there are many other kinds of noteworthy work experiences acquired through activities outside of the place of employment. For example, those who do volunteer work may have gained valuable experience in image building, fund raising, or client services. Giving of one's time and talent to charitable organizations demonstrates commitment and character. Experiences gained through such activities should be included in your resume.

Availability:

A prospective employee must be available to begin work within a reasonable period of time. Usually this is stated in the job announcement. Indeed, availability is readiness. However, you must be cautious about being over-eager to take the first opportunity and suspend the search prematurely.

Reliability:

It seems that showing up prepared is 87% of life. A person who is on time and is prepared to carry out the mission is reliable. He or she is a bottom line person and is consistently dependable. Be sure to point out in your work history how you have demonstrated reliability.

Physical Limitations:

The Americans with Disabilities Act (ADA) of 1990, prohibits discrimination against qualified individuals with disabilities. There are occasions when a bonafide occupational qualification allows discrimination, since an individual may not be qualified to carry out the work tasks. For example, if a job requires lifting 40-pound packages all day, it is understandable that not everyone is capable of doing such strenuous work. A realistic job preview will reveal any potential physically challenging work.

Interpersonal Skills:

A self-evaluation of your interpersonal skills is a worthwhile exercise. Most of us assume that we are indeed effective with our communication skills and if someone doesn't understand us then they must have a problem. A few types of interpersonal communications skills follow. Specifically, reflective listening, logical consequences, descriptive recognition, conflict management, collaborative problem solving, and nonverbal awareness. Each of these skills is briefly discussed to serve as a reminder of the intricate communication process. It should be noted that some or all of these practices may be interjected during the interview process.

Reflective Listening:
Reflective listening demonstrates an active role in the listening process. You may offer immediate feedback to the speaker by restating your interpretation of what was said. For example,

> Joe: *"Ed, we're looking for a job candidate who can use the popular software packages as an integral part of his or her work."*
>
> Ed: *"By popular software do you mean word processing, database and spreadsheets?"*
>
> Joe: *"Yes, but graphics software familiarity is also desirable."*
>
> Ed: *"I am quite familiar with each of those software packages."*

Joe and Ed had a meaningful dialogue, largely because of Ed's reflective listening technique.

Logical Consequences:
Logical consequences serve well as an interpersonal communication tool that is appropriate to use when it is necessary to remind someone of the outcome of an action or inaction. For example, a segment of a realistic job preview follows:

Steve: "Kris, timely and accurate completion of work assignments is critical to your success and our success. A person unable to meet deadlines has no place in our organization."

Kris: "I understand, and I am not averse to a pressure cooker environment. I enjoy the dynamics and the challenge of a focused organization."

Kris made it very clear that she understands the working conditions and welcomes the opportunity to be a part of a fast-paced workplace.

Descriptive Recognition:

Descriptive recognition serves to enhance the communication process by specifically pointing out one's understanding of events. For example,

Bob: "Thanks for the interview and considering me as a finalist for the job. You said that you expect to make your decision by next Wednesday. Do you think that I will be informed of your decision by next Friday?"

Succinctly, Bob said thanks, reaffirmed that a job candidate selection will be made next week, and asked a question in regard to notification of results at a specific point in time.

Conflict Management:

Everyone who has experienced conflict knows the feelings of winning and losing. Most Americans have been brought up to be winners. Sometimes winning an argument is more important than being right or wrong. When conflict is present, anxieties are high. If either party forces a win/lose scenario, then it will result in a lose/lose proposition. Even if a person "wins" an argument the matter is not over. Generally, the "loser" will become preoccupied with how to even up the score. Mutual respect of opinion will help to alleviate destructive feuding and will diffuse the conflict enabling a constructive win/win conclusion.

Invariably, during the interview process for managerial positions two questions are standard fare: (1) How do you handle conflict on the job? and (2) How would you describe your management style? Anticipating these questions and developing some well thought out responses could yield better odds of you getting the job.

Collaborative Problem Solving:

It is important to reflect on your problem solving abilities. Collaborative problem solving is the essence of the "new" management or teamwork philosophy. If people choose to work together for the good of their organization, then problems may be solved not at the expense of others, but rather with complementary mutually satisfactory results.

Nonverbal Awareness:

As communicators we receive and transmit messages nearly all of the time. We are usually cognizant of the signals being sent by others, sometimes it's through body language and other times through innuendoes. Being able to read and react to these nonverbal communication signals is an important part of interpersonal skills and is especially important during the interview process. A human resource manager of a large textile company tells of his "test" for prospective employees. After the usual interview dialogue, he informs the candidate that overtime is expected and is frequently needed. If the candidate has a negative reaction, such as squirming or a blank stare, then the individual is rejected from further consideration. Conversely, a person who willingly embraces overtime as an opportunity is further considered for the job. In this case, nonverbal awareness is used to screen out job candidates.

Appearance:

Appearance is your packaging. Of course, grooming, clothing, and fashion that is appropriate for the occasion, comprise the statement of your unspoken professionalism. A manager of a utility company cites the case of the man or woman who is well groomed, wearing a business suit, carrying a professional attaché, and having unpolished shoes. This is the person to whom the human resource manager refers to as almost well dressed. This may be an indicator of the attitude of the job candidate and relate to his or her work standards—almost good enough. Remember there is no mind police force or legislation to eliminate such nonverbal biases.

Special Skills:

Your skills that are especially appropriate to the job should be highlighted in a cover letter when applying for a position. Special skills should be discussed in response to job responsibilities. For example, if an announced job states that computer literacy is required, then specifically point out in your cover letter how you are qualified. List languages and software with which you are familiar and demonstrate how you effectively used your computer skills in the past, either in or outside of the workplace.

Your Self-Promotion

Personal selling, advertising, public relations, and generating options are all areas that may be exploited for career pursuits. A listing of opportunities to explore for your promotional activities follows.

Table 4-2
SELF-PROMOTION
Windows of Opportunity

PERSONAL SELLING	PUBLIC RELATIONS
Networking	Announcements
Associations	Business Cards
	Volunteer Work
ADVERTISING	**GENERATING OPTIONS**
Resume	Placement Tests
Cover Letter	World Wide Web Inquiries
Letters of Inquiry	Transition Center Services
Headhunters	Organizations of Specific Groups

Personal Selling:
Basically, personal selling is self-promotion. It is something that you must do, and do without guilt. After all, if a business didn't sell its products, then it wouldn't survive in our market driven economy. Selling is an integral part of the free enterprise system. You are an entity. Start selling!

Networking:

Networking might include exchanging job lead information with colleagues at work or outside of the workplace. Promotion through speaking engagements, or contacts developed as a result of leadership roles in charitable organizations, where your words are seen by others as a stimulus to action, are valuable sources of potential job opportunities.

Scenario 4-1

Networking: Client Case

An accountant lost his job because of downsizing. The manager of the local gas station casually asked how he was one day while servicing the car. The accountant admitted he had been unemployed for several weeks. The manager asked about his work and the accountant described the specialty tasks he carried out. The station manager immediately gave the accountant his wife's office telephone number with the encouragement that her company was looking for someone with his experience and credentials. He got the job and was working the following week!

Networking can also be accomplished through the mail—or email. A laid off administrator for a national church office created a monthly newsletter, consisting of one page, that he sent to his "network." He included the position he was seeking, his list of accomplishments and other resume type details. When he finally landed an offer that he accepted, his final newsletter was a "thank you" to all. Many wrote or called to say they were pleased he found work, but they would miss hearing from him. Therefore, he continued to send an annual letter. Keep the newsletter alive for the next job search!

Associations:

Membership in associations can be an invaluable resource for networking and may result in job leads. Participating in the governance of the association is yet another way to demonstrate leadership strengths to the membership.

Advertising:

Advertising may include: a fine-tuned resume; an innovative job specific cover letter; letters of inquiry; or use of headhunters' services.

Your Resume:

Your resume is you in written form. It must be carefully prepared and ideally should be tailored to the job for which you are applying, so don't rely on a quick copy service to do this for you. Advice on resume writing is fine, but it's your life, you know it, so you write it. Remember, generally the resume is the closest to perfection a person will ever become.

Everything on your resume should reflect what you hope to do in the future. Highlight activities you want to repeat in your next job. If you know how to prepare a budget but hope to never do it again, then don't put that on your resume. You are marketing your best self, so don't sell what you don't want to do anymore. This will increase your chances of making a good employment match. For your reference, there is an example of a resume and cover letter in Appendix 1.

Cover Letter:

The cover letter is what the reader sees first. It's their first impression of you. Be certain that it is outstanding! If there is a job announcement, write to it. Say how you are qualified to do the job and why you welcome the opportunity. Use specific examples that clearly demonstrate your successes with stipulated job requirements.

Letters of Inquiry:
When expressing interest about job opportunities in an organization you should clearly state why you are interested in working for that enterprise. You may cite company specific favorable newspaper or trade journal articles on such subjects as new construction, plant expansion, workforce increase, products or services sold, or market share expansion. Express interest and offer a resume. Include a question at the end of your letter. This is more likely to generate a response to your inquiry.

Headhunters:
These are fee-paid job searchers. These firms will help you find a job, but remember they serve as agents. Be sure to know in advance the details of the fee arrangement. These fees may be paid by the employer or the employee. The amount could be a substantial portion of first year's earnings.

Scenario 4-2

Headhunter: Client Case
An employed woman who wanted to get into the training field arranged to visit a headhunter who recruited for local companies in the field of human resources. The "hunter" was considered the premier source for quality applicants. During the discussion, the recruiter listed the qualities, credentials and experience that she looked for when presenting a candidate.

Highlight Your Many Values

The career changer used that list to create professional development goals and spent the next two years learning new skills and generating opportunities to offer training in her organization and with professional associations at local, regional and state conferences. After rewriting her resume, she returned to the headhunter's office and was greeted enthusiastically. She had developed exactly what was required. The headhunter never landed a job offer for the career changer, but she found opportunities on her own that were made possible by that development plan, which was a direct result of an interview with a headhunter.

Public Relations:

Public relations, or PR, may be gained with memberships in associations and through committee or interest group meetings. News releases of accomplishments, such as writing an article or leading a fund raising event for a charitable organization, are valuable and will provide positive public relations for you.

Scenario 4-3

Public Relations: Client Case

A trailing spouse found herself relocated from a large metropolitan area with many contacts to a small town not knowing a soul. Her perusal of the Chamber of Commerce membership book indicated that there would be few opportunities for her intended role of business consultant.

She asked the Chamber to recommend ways to get to know the business owners. They asked her to offer a workshop in their business development series and suggested she contact the editor of the local business journal.

The workshop was publicized in all the Chamber publications, was well attended, and she landed two contracts from one program. In addition, the editor of the business journal invited her to write a monthly column on business topics for six months. They were all published with her picture. A year later she enjoys a modest income from the consulting generated from those two efforts. It was more than she hoped for from such a small community.

Announcements:

When seeking new opportunities, one option is to generate a mailing list of individuals or businesses that may be interested in news of your availability in the job market, as a prospective employee or as a consultant. The announcement may include information of the location of an office that you have established (it may be a home office) and the services that you provide.

Business Cards:

A personal business card should include your name, telephone and fax numbers, e-mail address, and mailing address. It need not include a title or a current employer. However, your specialty or profession should be indicated. For example,

| Mary Smith, MBA |
| *Financial Analyst* |

P.O. Box 3456	e-mail msmith.aol.com
Hopesville, NY	Telephone and Fax
71177	711-642-6789

Highlight Your Many Values 77

Printing business cards requires only a small cash investment. You must have a business card. Carefully consider how you want to describe yourself. Consider listing your favorite professional activity, even if no one has hired you to do it yet full time. Just be sure you have some experience.

This is a good tactic for the career shifter. If you want to move from training administration to training delivery and all your experience has been at professional meetings and as a volunteer—use it! You are describing your next job.

Volunteer Work:

Volunteering your time to charitable organizations provides a valuable service to the enterprise, its clients, and you. An added benefit may be experience to add to your resume. For example, volunteering your services to contribute to the development of a management information system may give you a competitive edge in the job market. It's OK to think about getting something in return for giving. All parties win. Plus, the interaction with committee and board members sets the stage for further long-range networking benefits. Volunteer to learn a new skill or use a favorite skill to the benefit of others. Then your accomplishment will provide additional support in your job search.

Scenario 4-4

Volunteer Work: Client Case
An academic administrator wished to learn more about organizational finance, so she volunteered to be the treasurer of a hospital auxiliary. She learned bookkeeping, budgeting, and financial analysis by working with a CPA who served as an

auditor. This new knowledge and ability helped her secure her next job in the business world. The switch from academia to business is a tough one and she knew the financial experience would add to her promotional package. It worked!

Generating Options:

This is an area were "innovativeness" is given new meaning. In the "new" economy, it seems that a pioneer spirit is needed for success in our new century. Some examples of generating options are: placement tests; World Wide Web inquiries; and exploring/exploiting career transition center services.

Scenario 4-5

Generating Options: Client Case

A retail administrator wanted to change jobs because she was feeling dissatisfied with her current responsibilities and tasks. She obtained an interview for a position managing a community education center for a local hospital. It would give her a chance to work outside the retail industry and still allow her to use her educational background. It seemed an ideal opening for moving into an education environment. Prior to the scheduled interview, the Human Resource recruiter asked her to review the position description. As she read it, she realized that the administrative duties required for the job were what she clearly wanted to avoid.

She called the recruiter and stated that she was not really interested in pursuing the job. She apologized and asked that the appointment be canceled. It seemed more honest than going through the interview process knowing she would not accept the offer, if made. The recruiter was curious and asked what she was looking for. She replied that she would love to be conducting training programs, not handling the administrative details. Fortuitously, the hospital had just approved a new position, Training Manager for staff, and she was invited to apply. She landed the job and loved it.

Placement Tests:

Exploring possibilities through such approaches as taking examinations offered by various state or federal governmental agencies may result in a variety of job options. Usually, these options are generated over a lengthy period of time. However, these efforts may ultimately lead to a series of job offers.

World Wide Web Inquiries:

Another approach is to use the internet and the world wide web to explore employment opportunities. For example, on the world wide web, the address for America's Job Bank is: www.ajb.dni.us. It provides many windows to different job offers. Appendix 2 contains a listing of World Wide Web sites that are very useful for conducting a job search. Additional sites are presented in Chapter 6. Still another option is to set up a home page on the internet. If you subscribe to an online system such as America on Line or AT&T, you may set up a home page that describes your expertise and interests. This may lead to inquiries from prospective employers or possibly entrepreneurs who may be seeking partners.

Transition Center Services:

A transition center may be managed by the employer or by a private consulting firm. Typically, the services that are provided by transition centers include career counseling, interview workshops, resume preparation, word processing, job inquiries through the internet, and job referral assistance.

Job seekers should take advantage of the many services offered by transition centers. One career transition center in the Northeast offers a cafeteria style approach to those in need of job search assistance. This particular center lists an agenda of activities complete with date, time, and topic. Some topics typically included are: dealing with the loss of your job; goal setting; resume writing; cover letter writing; effective use of the internet; interview preparation; salary negotiations; and job options.

Organizations of Specific Groups:

A number of agencies serve the needs of specific groups of people. Six populations of the workforce are presented in Table 4-3 together with the organization from which you may gather detailed information.

Table 4-3
Workforce Populations–Specific Groups

OLDER WORKERS

Contact	**Address**
The National Association of Older Workers Employment Services	409 3rd St., SW Suite 200 Washington, DC 20024
American Association of Retired Persons Workforce Program Department	601 East St., NW Floor A5 Washington, DC 20049

National Caucus/Center on Black Aged, Inc.	1424 K St., NW Suite 500 Washington, DC 20005
National Association for Hispanic Elderly	2727 West 6th St. Suite 270 Los Angles, CA 90057

DISABLED PERSONS

Contact	**Address**
President's Committee on Employment of People With Disabilities	1331 F St. NW 3rd Floor Washington, DC 20004

MINORITIES

Contact	**Address**
National Association for the Advancement of Colored People (NAACP)	4805 Mount Hope Dr. Baltimore, MD 21215

THE BLIND

Contact	**Address**
Job Opportunities for the Blind (JOB) National Federation of the Blind	1800 Johnson St. Baltimore, MD 21230

VETERANS

Contact	**Address**
Veterans' Employment and Training Services (VETS)	200 Constitution Ave., NW S-1315 Washington, DC 20210

WOMEN

Contact	Address
U.S. Department of Labor Women's Bureau	200 Constitution Ave., NW Washington, DC 20210
Wider Opportunities for Women	815 15th St., NW Suite 916 Washington, DC 20005

Your Place

This is where you are willing to work. In some cases, it may mean a re-location. A re-location may be a matter of commuting or an outright move. An extreme example of relocating yourself, but not your family, is when your job is in Los Angles and your residence is in New York. Relocating may well be one of the toughest decisions that you have to make in your job search. There are so many considerations relating to a move. Do you move yourself, but not your family? Will you set up two households? What about the increased costs? A non-exhaustive checklist of issues to consider for the big decision of relocating follows in Table 4-4.

Table 4-4
QUESTIONS TO ANSWER FOR A
NEW PLACE DECISION

Can I commute rather than re-locate?

What about my spouse's job—and income?

How will the move impact upon the kids (school, friends, activities, etc.)?

How good are the schools at the new location?

Is the cost of living more or less, where the new job is located?

What is the tax structure—how will it impact upon my overall cost of living?

What is the quality of living compared to where I am now?

What is the predominant lifestyle—urban, suburban, rural, country?

Is there a college degree in progress for me or my spouse—can it be finished without a residency requirement?

How are the overall employment opportunities in the geographic area under consideration?

Are quality day care facilities available—at what cost?

Are there services conveniently located—shopping centers, grocery stores, etc.?

Are there adequate health care facilities for my family's needs?

What is the prime transportation system?

How much is the relocation cost?—Who will pay?

Is the weather dramatically different from what I am accustomed to?

What kind of culture will I have to become acclimated to?

≈ ≈ ≈

Your Price

The subject of price includes both objective and subjective dimensions. After determining what is truly needed for sustaining your lifestyle of choice, the dollars needed to keep the ship afloat may be objectively measured. The subjective dimension includes ego involvement, particularly of self-worth. It may be difficult to accept a pay decrease of $10,000, even if there is no connection between the cut in pay and the money required for maintaining your chosen lifestyle. With any discussion of price, a reality check is in order. Overall, today's job market is still operating within a scaresizing mentality. Employees, whether unionized or not, are not demanding big pay increases. Typically, increases range from negative amounts (give backs) to 3%. Many employers have dumped workers with years on the job, in favor of younger workers, because of the windfall of immediate wage expense reductions and less benefit cost. Although age discrimination legislation prevents unfair practices based on age, there are many ways that some organizations choose to circumvent the law. For example, some organizations eliminate jobs, then reengineer the jobs and hire new people to fill the new positions. In any event, the bottom line has the same meaning to the unemployed—probably, starting pay will be less than the prior job. Of course, starting pay is contingent on the industry and specific companies within the industry.

Some of the meanings of the word "price" follow.

Table 4-5
YOUR PRICE

Salary	Personal Time
Overtime	Travel Reimbursement
Health Care	Living Expenses
Cost of Living Increases	Day Care
Retirement Plan	Relocation Payments
Education Incentives	Cafeteria Benefits Plan
Vacation Time	Retrenchment Plan

Salary:

After a realistic review of your economic needs to sustain your lifestyle you are positioned to discuss salary needs. Just remember the job market is very competitive, so the entry salary is not necessarily the most important part of the decision. For example, opportunities for promotion and subsequent pay increases may be much more significant. Expectations should be based not entirely on your past pay level, but based on an entire package. If company A offers fully paid health care coverage and company B requires a 50% contribution, then company A's plan may be $2,500 more generous than company B's. Yet another consideration in the compensation package is an incentive bonus plan. Be sure to learn the details of the plan including the criteria to achieve such an award. Also, you need to know how successful performance might convert into a dollar amount. Some bonus plans are based on company performance, such as profitability. Others are completely arbitrary and defy any logic as to a basis of award.

Overtime:

The issue of overtime is sometimes more complex than just occasionally working over 40 hours a week. Some businesses require employees to work overtime on a regular basis. One human resources manager confided that his most important question to prospective employees is: "What are your feelings about working overtime?" If the job candidate reacts negatively in any way, verbal or nonverbal, the individual kisses good-bye any hope for the job. The company's position is that overtime, as needed, is cheaper than hiring more workers. Consequently, it requires all employees to be not only willing to put in the extra hours, but to do so gladly. This is an example of a business with a culture of overtime expectancy.

Health Care:

Health care, including medical and dental coverage, is probably the largest value benefit that an employee needs to be concerned with. Along with job security, health care costs are one of the top priority issues negotiated during collective bargaining activities. Family health care plans cost in the range of $4,000 to $5,500 per year. Contingent upon your tax bracket, it means that you may have to earn about $7,000 in before tax dollars to purchase your own health care coverage. The point is clearly made that this is one benefit of significant value. When an employer pays, all or part of it, you should consider this amount as part of the compensation package.

Cost of Living Increases:

Cost of living increases or pay raises to keep up with inflation (and perhaps get ahead) are automatic in some companies. Others take a wait and see approach to what, if any, pay increases may be demanded by employees. If the workers are unionized, the collective bargaining agreement will spell out the terms of pay increases over the life of the contract. Management and labor will negotiate in "good faith" (according to labor law) prior to termination of the current contract. If the workers are not unionized, then precedent coupled with current trends probably will continue.

Retirement Plan:

If you are so fortunate as to have been fully vested in a retirement plan from a former job, then perhaps the new employer's plan is not so significant to you. In any event, whatever the offering, tax deferred plans are helpful for sheltering income. Most downsized workers are in need of further preparation for retirement. A company that offers a paid plan or dollar-for-dollar matching plan can add up to tremendous value over time. Whatever the plan, its value should be considered as part of the overall economic package.

Education Incentives:

There are other non-salary items for pay package assessment. Tuition reimbursement plans for employees and possibly their family members may satisfy specific needs. One woman accepted a job at a university at a pay rate much lower than other offers, but a benefit offered was free tuition for employees and their families. She was allowed to take courses to finish her master's degree and her son was granted a full tuition waiver. The tuition was $14,000 per year, a value of $56,000 over four years! Think about the dollars that would have to be earned before taxes to pay out that sum of money.

Vacation Time:

Vacation time is probably the last thing on your mind if you've been unemployed, but is still another factor in the compensation equation. As a new hire you will probably have to go through a time cycle to build up time off with pay. Unfortunately, this may be quite a contrast from your last job. Maybe you had attained 5 weeks off with pay because of your longevity in the former job. Now you're back to square one. You must work 12 months before you will be granted 1 week vacation time. Sure it's an issue, perhaps you can negotiate, but chances are that other job candidates would joyfully accept these conditions.

Personal Time:

Personal time is another factor that may mean more to some than others. For example, a primary care giver to an ill child or parent would need more flexibility in terms of time off than one who has no such responsibilities. There has been recent legislation to require employers to allow employees time off to manage such needs. Pay may not be the issue, since the paid personal time may be restricted to a certain number of hours or days per year. Discrimination laws notwithstanding, a question that emerges from such circumstances is, would a business knowingly hire someone so burdened?

Highlight Your Many Values

Travel Reimbursement:

Transportation reimbursement is offered by some companies that require travel. After all, if you have to travel on your job and you are not fully reimbursed for related costs, then your absorption of these costs (less taxes) must be subtracted from your compensation package.

Living Expenses:

Living expenses are sometimes offered as a sweetener when an employee is relocated to a different part of the country or to a country outside of the U.S. For example, an employee may be encouraged to move to and live in the Middle East if the incentives are many. Housing for the employee and his or her family, travel, food, education, and entertainment, may be some of the costs that are paid by the employer. Obviously, this would add up to a very large percentage of the base pay.

Day Care:

A rising need and ever increasing cost is quality day care. The needs for day care are especially prevalent in families where both parents work. Also, inner city businesses have unique needs for providing day care for young women who have kids, but can't afford baby sitters or day care costs. If a business truly needs the workers from these populations, then it must compromise and offer benefits that it might otherwise not even consider. Day care costs may range from $80 to over $350 per week.

Relocation Payments:

Relocation payments are very helpful if a major move is required. Some employers are willing to cover these costs as an incentive to bring a recruit on-board. Of course, this demonstrates good will on the part of the employer. The cost of such a move may have a value of $4,000 or more.

Cafeteria Benefits Plan:

A so-called "cafeteria" benefits plan is extremely useful for a couple when both spouses work. You may choose certain benefits so that there is not duplicate coverage. This prevents a waste factor that contributes virtually no additional benefit to the employee. Let's use an example where both working spouses have health care coverage with different employers. This couple should have coverage with one company, perhaps the one that pays full cost. If a cafeteria style benefits program exists, then the other spouse may choose not to have the duplicate health coverage, but instead choose to collect the equivalent dollar value of the benefit or some other compensation such as time off. There is no additional cost to the employer and it certainly keeps the employee happy.

Retrenchment Plan:

Retrenchment plans are structured courses of action to be implemented if a company decides to downsize. Generally, the plan would detail how the shrinkage would occur. Who would go, who would stay, what positions would be eliminated, and what markets, if any, would be sacrificed. The human resource factor of retrenchment plans may be spelled out in a collective bargaining agreement and is generally based on seniority, unless positions or departments are eliminated.

So, price considerations are made up of much more than the base salary. As illustrated earlier, each component of the compensation package or your price should be considered. A worksheet in summary format for your reference follows in Table 4-6.

Table 4-6
WORKSHEET FOR COMPENSATION PACKAGE ANALYSIS 1

Annualized Value

Item	Former Job	New Job	Variance
Salary	$	$	$
Overtime			
Health Care			
Cost of Living Increases			
Retirement Plan			
Education Incentives			
Vacation Time			
Personal Time			
Travel Reimbursement			
Living Expenses			
Day Care			
Relocation Payments			
Cafeteria Benefits Plan			
Retrenchment Plan			
Other			
Total Values			

An Example of Annualizing a Compensation Package

Let's assume that Cynthia Tilden lost her job three months ago. She was a computer support specialist in the banking industry and was making $42,000 annual salary, plus given health care benefits at 50% of cost. She had accrued seven days personal time (the maximum), and two weeks vacation. She was paid the equivalent value of this time when she was laid off. Cynthia has a two-year old daughter and has been paying $85 per week for day care. Ms. Tilden was offered a similar job with a company located in a neighboring state. She has a tough decision to make because if she moves she would have to become re-established with housing, familiar with the locale, and redefine her social interests. Also, she would have to sacrifice the convenience of proximity to family and friends. Assuming that Cynthia has thought through all of the social concerns and concluded that the move makes sense, we will now take a look at the economic side of the equation (Table 4-7).

A quick analysis of Cynthia's job offer reveals that although her base starting pay is $9,000 less than her last job, her overall compensation package is $9,015 higher. In her previous job, company policy prohibited overtime. Cynthia was assured that overtime was an option rather than a demand in the new position and she feels that $5,000 is a reasonable expectation, since the overtime rate is double the hourly base rate.

Health care is 100% paid with the new company. This adds an increase of $2,250 to her compensation package. Of course, the benefit of not having these dollars taxed makes this plan even more attractive. The new job offer includes an automatic 3% pay increase per year and is increased contingent upon inflation. The previous job offered no pay increases for the next two years and it was expected that the next pay raise would be 1.5%.

Table 4-7
WORKSHEET FOR COMPENSATION PACKAGE ANALYSIS 2

Annualized Value

Item	Former Job	New Job	Variance
Salary	$42,000	$33,000	($9,000)
Overtime	0	5,000	5,000
Health Care	2,250	4,500	2,250
Cost of Living Increases	0	990	990
Retirement Plan	840	3,300	2,460
Education Incentives	0	2,000	2,000
Vacation Time	1,615	2,538	923
Personal Time/ Sick Time	1,131	1,523	392
Travel Reimbursement	0	500	500
Living Expenses	0	0	0
Day Care	0	3,000	3,000
Relocation Payments	0	0	0
Cafeteria Benefits Plan	0	500	500
Retrenchment Plan	0	0	0
Other			
Total Values	$47,836	$56,851	$9,015

The job under consideration offers a retirement fund contribution of 10% of base salary. This compares favorably with Cynthia's prior plan, which was 2% of salary. She was offered three weeks vacation for each of the first 5 years of employment and then, an additional 1 week per year worked thereafter, up to a maximum of 8 weeks per year.

The personal and/or sick time offered is a slightly better plan than what she had before, so she added the $392 difference to her analysis. The new company offers an incentive to use public transportation whenever possible with an allowance of $500 per year. She believes that she would be able to take advantage of this offer.

An outstanding benefit with the new company is an on-site day care center that she is free to use each workday. Since she would no longer have to pay for this service, she estimated the value at $3,000. Again, it would be valued much higher if she considered after tax earnings to yield the $3,000.

Finally, there is a cafeteria benefits plan arrangement where she will opt for an additional pay amount of $500 at the end of the year in lieu of seasonal tickets to the local professional football games (she can't stand football).

Upon analysis, the results are clear. A job listed at $9,000 less than one's last salary is not necessarily cause to reject an offer. Learn all of the details. It just might be a much better deal than you had in your last job.

Summary:

This chapter provides methods for analysis of you as a valuable product and offers suggestions on how to promote yourself, think through various place considerations, and how to determine your price.

You may want to consider a variety of critical questions relating to your job inquiries. Some important questions follow in Table 4-8.

Table 4-8
QUESTIONS TO ANSWER FOR JOB PLANNING

What is the nature of the work?

Is the job compatible with my intermediate needs, objectives, and my long-term goals?

What are the characteristics of the job in terms of work week hourly scheduling?

Are hours regular or irregular?

Is travel required?

Do employees tend to stay with the company?

What are the opportunities for pay increases, promotion, and job security?

All things considered, will the job being assessed improve not only my immediate situation, but benefit me in the longer term?

Appendix 1

Job Announcement, Cover Letter, and Resume

Ellen Wu is interested in the job that was announced in the local newspaper on June 2. She has the appropriate academic credentials and she feels that she has enough experience to qualify for the job.

Help Wanted
Human Resources
Generalist

Leading health care services company, is seeking a Human Resources Generalist with an excellent track record.

You will consult with business managers in such areas as employee relations, coaching and counseling employees, staffing, performance management, compensation, and change management. Also, your duties will include outplacement services.

The ideal candidate will have a minimum of 3 years experience as a generalist. Strong interpersonal skills are needed. Working knowledge of compensation and incentive compensation plans is a must. Ability to interact with all levels of management and hourly employees is necessary.

Personal computer skills are required. A BS/BA in business administration or human resources management or equivalent experience will be acceptable.

We offer a very competitive compensation package, outstanding benefits and an opportunity for growth in a team oriented work environment.

Please send your resume in confidence to:
AD # 961
Box 57927
Franklin, MO 27901

Ellen has decided to respond to the advertisement. Her letter of inquiry and resume follow.

The Cover Letter

June 3, 200x

AD # 961
Box 57927
Franklin, MO 27901

Dear Human Resources Manager:

    I am very interested in the Human Resources Generalist position described in yesterday's Franklin Gazette newspaper.
    I have worked in the health care industry for the past three and one-half years as an Assistant Human Resources Manager. One of my job duties was to assist employees who were to be "out-placed." Ironically, I am now following the advice that I had been giving. My position was eliminated as a result of corporate restructuring. I understand an organization's need to streamline operations and fully support efficiency of operations. Clearly, I now have a first hand understanding of out-placement from the perspective of the employee. This experience will help me to better serve the personal and professional needs of those whose positions will be eliminated.

My resume indicates a progressive work history of accomplishments. I have always enjoyed working with management personnel as well as hourly employees and have been referred to by my supervisor and others as the bridge of tranquillity between both groups. My performance evaluations have always rated my interpersonal skills as superior.

Last year, I had the opportunity to design an innovative pay plan that, in fact, helped increase productivity by 14% over the prior year. I thoroughly enjoyed that project and was pleased to be able to demonstrate outstanding success with a win/win compensation plan.

My computer skills are excellent and I keep current with the latest hardware and software packages by attending informational meetings, seminars, and training sessions.

My educational background includes an Associate Degree in Business Administration, a Bachelor of Science Degree in Business Administration, and I am enrolled in an MBA program with a major in Human Resource Management.

I believe that I am well prepared for the job of Human Resources Generalist with your organization and look forward to an interview.

I will call you next week to see if you need any additional information. I sincerely thank you for your consideration.

Very truly yours,

Ellen Wu

18 Marlin Avenue, Franklin, MO 27905
Telephone & Fax 516.437.8956 • Email: ewu@aol.com

**Resume of:
Ellen Wu**

Experience:

Medical A.I. Systems
January 1997 to April 200x

Assistant Human Resources Manager. Job duties included working with managers to implement self-directed work teams, mentoring, the recruitment and hiring process, design and installation of an innovative performance appraisal system. I was responsible for the development and implementation of a totally revised pay plan which was very successful as evidenced with a 14% productivity increase over the prior year. Other responsibilities included overall labor/management relations, compensation systems, and providing outplacement services. All of my work required computer application from basic word processing to sophisticated database management, to quantitative analysis of productivity and performance tracking. My job role was highly visible and required effective interpersonal skills.

Robotics, Inc.
June 1992 to January 1997

Employee Relations Specialist. Job duties included working with unionized employees on such matters as conflict resolution, grievance handling, and contract negotiations. This job provided me with a strong background in labor law as well as the collective bargaining process. I enjoyed my job and have a demonstrated record of success, but I left this job to pursue a broader role in the arena of Human Resource Management.

Education:
Associate in Science Degree in Business Administration, Bachelor of Science Degree in Business Administration, Master of Business Administration (candidate) in Human Resource Management.

Personal:
Enjoy hiking, water sports, running, and chess. I am a volunteer reading teacher for illiterate adults and participate in fund raising campaigns for the American Red Cross.

References
Gladly furnished upon request.

Appendix 2

Job Inquiries

Checklist of addresses on the World Wide Web for the major job banks

America's Employers
www.americasemployers.com

America's Job Bank
www.ajb.dni.us

Career.Com
www.career.com

Career Mosaic
www.careermosaic.com

College Grad
www.collegegrad.com

Department of Labor
www.doleta.gov

Employment Guide
www.employmentguide.com

Go Jobs
www.gojobs.com

Head Hunter
www.headhunter.com

Hot Jobs
www.hotjobs.com

Job Options
www.joboptions.com

Jobs
www.jobs.com

Job Star
www.jobstar.com

Monster Board
www.monster.com

Net Temps
www.net-temps.com

Thingamajob
www.thingamajob.com

Chapter Five

> **LEARN FROM OTHERS**
>
> ❧❧❧
>
> **Course of Action Number 5**

Introduction

If you have read this far, we assume that you have been doing a fair amount of homework. Now, it is time to take all the information that you have gathered about yourself, and use it in a way that others have, to land your next work opportunity. Notice we did not say job.

❧ ❧ ❧

Your Options

The next step you take might have one of many looks to it. You might want to find a job in a company just like the one you left. You also could be looking for the same kind of work but in a different type of organization. Perhaps this is the time to start your own business. You might opt for a different approach by taking on a variety of contracts or part-time positions to complete your work profile. So you must decide which of these paths look best for you.

You may choose each of these routes on your future career path. You need to know there is no one right answer to the job search program. At different times on the path, various options will be the better choice. Keep in mind that you are only making a decision. If things do not work out, you need only make another decision.

Decisions are not right or wrong, they are just decisions. What makes for challenge, excitement and fulfillment, is knowing that you can always make another selection and just move on. But how do you know what is better at this time? Maybe a brief reminder of the decision making process would be helpful here.

❧ ❧ ❧

Decision Making Process

There are proven steps you can take, that will increase your satisfaction potential with your choice. The five steps that we will discuss are: Gather data; Analyze the data; Develop alternatives; Choose; and Evaluate.

Step One
Gather data:

You have spent time looking at yourself and what you have to offer in terms of experience and skills, your financial needs, and even the costs of moving vs. staying where you are. All this information is critical in finalizing your targeted search.

Step Two
Analyze the data:

It helps to have it all in one place and to be able to look at it as information that will support your choice.

At different times of your life, money needs vary. For example, before and after children finish college can make a big difference in your budget.

Consider each item on the listing that follows.

Table 5-1
ANALYZE THE DATA

1. Salary
2. Benefits
3. Location (includes neighborhood, schools, academic and cultural opportunities, housing, recreation, churches, etc.)
4. Kind of company or work environment
5. People you would work with
6. Balance of personal and work time
7. Work hours
8. Opportunity for advancement
9. Opportunity for professional growth and development
10. Opportunity to use your favorite skills
11. Job security
12. Commitment to community, professional or church groups
13. Any other data you have that is not included on this list.

As you can see, gathering the data is critical, but how you handle it is even more important. You must have as much information as possible to make a good decision. You must also make sure that how you use it is consistent with your values.

Step Three
Develop alternatives:

Now you are ready to develop and decide on work alternatives.

Alternative One:
Finding a job similar to the one you left:

Your contacts and work experience are the most important tools you have for this scenario. Keep in touch with your former coworkers. Your former supervisor may be able to help you develop leads. If you belong to a professional or trade organization, the members should be of invaluable assistance to you in identifying openings and opportunities.

How did you find the job you just left? Often people forget what worked in the past might work now. Perhaps you were successful at one time landing a job from a classified newspaper ad. Most books on the job search will suggest that you avoid using the newspaper exclusively. But people do get hired from the paper. What worked before can work again. Just be sure to use several options and do not just depend on the classified ads.

If you graduated from a trade school, specialized college program, or are licensed or certified, you can contact affiliated associations for further leads. Your previous connections are usually all you need to reach the right people. Call. Write after you call. Avoid writing only.

Be careful not to put all your efforts in only one direction. The suggestion here is that you use all of the above options, not just one.

Alternative Two:
Locating the same kind of job in a different kind of organization:

Perhaps you worked for a large corporation and now would prefer a smaller company. You might want to move from profit to not-for-profit, or from not-for-profit to profit. You may want to put your work efforts into an organization that matches your values.

In each of these cases, you are not looking for different work, only a different environment. Your updated resume will probably be fine. The target organizations will be looking for someone with your experience and skills.

Scenario 5-1

Big and Small Apples: Client Case
- A young woman in advertising had a successful career in a well-respected Manhattan advertising firm. She really loved the work she did but found the lifestyle in New York too stressful. The commute, the cost of living, the long hours that the company demanded, all contributed to her eventual dissatisfaction on the job.
- She carried out some research on firms located in other large cities and finally decided to move to Baltimore. Before she left New York, she had landed a comparable position in another well-regarded firm in the new location. They were thrilled to get an experienced professional with

Big Apple experience. She was thrilled to be working in a less tense environment.

Alternative Three:
Starting Your Own Business:
Perhaps you believe that you have the experience you need to create your own business. The idea of being your own boss may be very attractive. You would be in charge of the operation from start to end. No one else is responsible. Success or failure is all yours. Your background has prepared you with the skills and contacts you would need to begin. You may also have some savings you could invest for the start-up. Or you may have some supporters who would back you with a variety of resources to get you started. Have colleagues suggested that you should start your own business?

Many people who leave full time employment do start their own businesses. The success rate is not great. However, there are excellent sources of information you can access, thus help make you one of the success stories. Most Community Colleges have small business programs or offer courses for a modest fee. The local government may also have an economic development office that offers advice and support. The library is full of books and sample business plans to give you a start. We recommend, *The Book of Profit: Seven Steps to Success for Small Business* 2nd Edition 2001, available from Barnes & Noble at (www.bn.com), or from PACT Publications at (www.pact-pub.com). Probably the best person to talk with would be someone you personally know who has already accomplished what you hope to do yourself.

If it sounds like we are suggesting more research, you are right. But why reinvent the wheel if you can go to the source and find excellent answers to your questions. Such sources may have answers to questions you have not even considered. Dig up and dig out all the information you can before beginning.

Scenario 5-2

Golden Oldies: Client Case

A young, married mother of one with the second child on the way, was notified by her company that they could only keep her on part-time after her maternity leave because of job re-engineering. There would be no benefits and the hours were inflexible. Upon reflection, she believed that there would be no gain to return.

She had been buying and refinishing antique furniture in her garage for years. She gave many completed pieces as gifts and used others in her home. At the time of her pregnancy, she was running out of space and the cash to continue buying. Her field was marketing. So her first step was to develop a feasibility plan for her "new business."

Her feasibility plan indicated that there was a market for the kind of country furniture she worked with and she found shared space in an antique row. Her marketing background served her well. She promoted her business effectively and her advertising paid off. At the end of her first year in business, she had enough profit to take care of all of her needs and to buy a new car. She used her professional skills in marketing along with her love of refinishing furniture to develop a successful enterprise that she fully enjoyed.

What she did not anticipate were the long hours involved in the business. At the end of the first year, her business was profitable enough to hire help, but most first year owners cannot count on this much "success."

Be sure that your boss (you) does not overwork you so that you burn out even though your business is expanding. Be prepared to take time off to keep your life balanced, knowing that you will still spend more hours at your own business, until you are well established, than you would as an employee.

The rewards of self-ownership are great but they come with a price. If it is one you can afford and choose wisely, you can work for yourself and love it.

Alternative Four:
Developing Contracts and Part-time Work:

One of the fastest growing work profiles is that of the self-employed independent contractor. This kind of work requires that the individual develop several sources of work, either simultaneously or sequentially. Rather than take a full time job with a single employer, they work part-time for several.

This may sound like another way to describe consulting. Consulting would fit this profile, of course. But it is not the only way to go. Also, consider working for a temporary agency. Just a few years ago temp agencies only supplied clerical type workers. That is no longer true. There are temp agencies who now provide CEO's on temporary contract. Almost every professional can find a temp agency that would be glad to have them on the books.

If you choose the temp agency route, you may receive benefits and they generally locate the work opportunities. Sometimes a temporary assignment can translate into a full time job offer, but that is the exception rather than the rule. Check the yellow pages and your professional or trade association to find out what is happening in your field. You should interview and discover the possibilities.

There are also some other benefits in this line of work. If you have the flexibility, you may elect to work full time for a period of time and then take some time off for travel, education or family plans. You can come back when you are ready and be reasonably assured of placement.

You may also wish to be a consultant. If you choose this avenue, you must factor in your marketing time. You will need to find your own work and this can take many hours. However, you can often be rehired by the company that laid you off. This is fairly common. Whether you consider this option may depend on your feelings toward the company as you leave. It may be difficult to return to the division you left. It may be hard to reconcile doing the same work without benefits. However, your hourly rate will generally be much higher than your previous employed rate, so you can budget for health care insurance, retirement, and marketing time.

The benefits of consulting are that you can choose how and where you want to work. You can develop some of those great ideas the company would not support and try them out on your clients. You can travel at someone else's expense to work at another location.

There will be times when no money is coming in so you must plan for this scenario, as you would for starting your own business selling goods or services. There are books on how to promote your consulting practice. You may be able to take a seminar or workshop on the nuts-and-bolts of consulting. As we mentioned in all the other options, you must do some homework to identify the pluses and pitfalls of the plan. You will need a good financial plan to keep you solvent during start-up and during the periods when you are not working, but seeking clients.

Scenario 5-3

Paradise Island: Client Case

A business consultant got his start while working at a full-time job and teaching part-time at the local University. One of his students was working for a company that needed some Organizational Development (OD). The instructor was teaching the basics of OD and the student, who was responsible for locating the consultant for his employer, was impressed. A few after-class discussions led to an interview. An offer was made that was very attractive. They wanted someone to consult in Jamaica, during the winter months, with a new division. The part-time professor was excited at the prospect of travel to a warm climate during the winter as well as working in a different culture. The pay was excellent. He decided to leave his full-time job to try it. The contract, which was not full-time, extended over many years. He continued to teach and continued to attract more contracts through his working students. He never promoted his consulting, but his skills were evident in the classroom and spoke for themselves. After 10 years, he continues to be successful. He loves the winter travel and is able to extend his stays for vacation. Sounds wonderful, especially if you're reading this in the winter and it is cold where you are!

Often consulting is an opportunity that is within your grasp from where you are right now. If this is an appealing alternative, it is never too early to begin planting the seeds for bringing a consulting job to fruition. Take on some internal consulting jobs in your current position. Offer to be on special task forces to develop new ideas or

Learn From Others 113

problem solve. It gives you new skills and makes you visible in the company and maybe even outside.

Scenario 5-4

Take the $ Train: Client Case
One of the big health insurance companies decided to implement a restructuring. A training manager in Human Resources volunteered to chair the task force on how to train employees in the new structure and work flow processes. He and his team came up with a winning program that earned acclaim from the executives. He sent a proposal to a professional conference selection committee, and his program was accepted. There were representatives from dozens of companies at his presentation. As a result of that conference, he earned several contracts for consulting. He reduced his hours at his company to part-time so that he could become a full time consultant. Eventually, offers from outside sources made it impossible to continue with his original company. Of course, they also hired him back for special projects. Everyone was a winner.

Are We Having Any Fun Yet?:
Once we spoke to an older, retired gentleman who had hated his job for the last 20 years he was in it. Asked why he did not leave it for something he liked, he responded that, "work was work." He did it to support his family. No one ever told him that he was supposed to enjoy his job. Although he always performed well, and he was praised for his many accomplishments, and was respected by his colleagues, he left every morning with a sense of dread—for 20 years!

You have a choice. You can find work that will allow you to use your 2000 or so hours per year at work performing functions that bring some degree of fulfillment.

When you leave, or when you are asked to move out of a job that you do not like, you are making space for someone else who may love that work. You are also giving yourself the opportunity to pursue your own dream. Life is not a dress rehearsal; this is it and you want to make it the best show possible.

Virtually all the employees we interviewed after reduction in workforce programs reported that they were leaving jobs they no longer liked or never liked at all. Accounts from relocated workers indicate that a very high percentage found work that was more in keeping with their skills and values. Most were receiving at least what they were earning before. Even if they took jobs at a lower pay, often the benefits were better. The work was more to their liking so the difference in pay often did not result in any reduction in lifestyle.

Scenario 5-5

Doing the Right Thing: Client Case
A young man who had worked at an electronics firm for 10 years was laid off. He came to the outplacement office very angry. We waited for him to finish venting and to settle down. He finally blurted out that he hated his job. I suggested that maybe he was not mad but relieved that he had lost his job. He immediately smiled, laughed a little and said I was probably right. He had not had the courage to leave on his own. He made good money but was depressed and dreaded coming in every day. He said that Sundays were awful

because he began to think about coming in on Monday. He had become withdrawn and listless. The job was certainly not keeping him healthy.

As he began to talk about jobs he liked in the past, it was obvious that he loved working in purchasing. Born to shop—with other peoples' money. He had been well respected in his previous positions but had left because of lack of upward mobility to a management position.

When asked about what he wanted in a job, he honestly said he loved the work, but really did not long to be a manager. It was in this discussion that he realized how much he loved the research, locating the right vendors and making the internal customer happy. He reflected that during our discussion, and he recognized that managing other people was not a priority. Although that represented a move up the career ladder, it was not a good move for him, based on his interests and values.

He left that day to call the company he had worked for previously. They did not have a job but referred him to another company who hired him on the spot, based on the recommendation of his former employer. In three weeks, he had a new job. He was making slightly less than he had at the electronics company but loved going to work every day.

It is important to remember that compensation is not the only reward for working.

Step Four
Choose:

Now you have gone through the first three steps and you are ready to choose. You have reliable information. You have used tools to help you evaluate the various options. You know what kinds of opportunities are out there. Decide. Plan. Take action.

Keep in mind that you are only making a decision. You are not committing yourself to a life long destiny. The next step allows you to put the decision in perspective.

Step Five
Evaluate:

Once you have made your decision and taken action on that choice, you will need to reflect on how well that decision is working for you. In many cases, you will find that, having done all the homework, the decision will be advantageous. But not always.

Scenario 5-6

Playing at Work: Client Case

A young man had taken a job as a broker in his father's firm. He had every advantage, but was failing. He had the skills to be successful in the job but he hated approaching people and trying to sell them a product. We looked at what he really wanted to do with his time. He loved golf. It was his passion. We talked about earning a living in that field. His homework was to call the many contacts he already had and to find out about job opportunities. With some reluctance and cynicism, he began his informational interviewing.

He found that there were many ways to earn a living in that field. However, he also found that there was not much money offered in any of the jobs he explored. Most of the people who were working, either as professionals or in sales, were willing to take lower pay to do what they loved. He realized that he was not willing to do that. He and his wife grew up in financially secure families with many luxuries. He was not going to take a path that led to fun but no money. He loved being outside, learning new practices in the game, and socializing with fellow players. I asked how often he was playing now. He explained it had been over a year since his last game.

So he needed to be doing something he loved while he re-examined his work life. We talked about the possibility of playing on a regular basis just for his own enjoyment. Novel idea!! For some reason, he was depriving himself of a joyful experience because he was not doing well at work. This only deepens any sense of loss, increases depression, and certainly does not make it any easier to work harder for success.

So he went back to golf and rediscovered his enjoyment in life. It affected his family life, making him more pleasant to be around. He found that he could go into the office and not dread it so much. He found that his work with clients improved. He also went golfing with them. He used golf to create rapport and relationships. Once this rapport was established, he found it natural and easy to talk to them about his financial products. Over time, his earnings improved. As long as he took the time to develop a relationship with potential clients, he found he was successful.

> He was able to bring his love of golf to work and make it work for him!

Your ability to step back and analyze the success of your choices is critical. It is also important to remember that whatever you choose, you must revisit it at least annually when things are going well, and immediately if you sense a deterioration in your satisfaction level or performance.

One of our premises is that you will not be seeking a life long position but you will use the skills and tools you develop for work in a variety of settings during your work life. Therefore, you will have plenty of practice over the years using the steps we have suggested for your use.

Choose, knowing that you are choosing for now. You are taking advantage of what the world has to offer you now with the current circumstances. So keep your resume up to date. Do not neglect your supportive network. Stay active in your professional and trade associations. Be a mentor for others. Help works in both upward and downward directions. Continue your interest in life and all the changes it offers you. What will remain constant are your basic interests and skills. You can put them to use in more ways that you can choose in this life-time.

There is enough work in this country for everyone. Be open to all the opportunities that present themselves. Know how to evaluate each one. Stay true to yourself and do what you love. When you do what you love, you are competent and confident. Someone will pay you to do that work competently. And when you retire, be sure to continue doing it for a fee or for free, in a setting that you enjoy.

When you are doing work you hate, you are doing someone else's job. Get out of it and make it available for the person who wants it. Then find your own work so you can give back to the world the gifts you were born to use.

ଈ ଈ ଈ

End Note

We hope you find the material in this chapter helpful. All the suggestions and tools we recommended have a record of success. We also hope the cases provided will help you to move forward knowing that others have faced similar circumstances and found fulfillment.

ଈ ଈ ଈ

Chapter Six

> **PREPARE FOR A SOFT LANDING WHEN A LAYOFF IS IMMINENT**
>
> ≈≈≈
>
> **Course of Action Number 6**

Introduction

Thus far, we have discussed a regrouping and reengineering for reemployment. Now, let's take a look at the gut wrenching situation of those still employed as they watch the job slicing pendulum swing. It is a persistent and ever penetrating motion that may take several months or just a few weeks before the cut.

Layoff is imminent! You're out, but you may not be sure exactly when. Let's examine this dilemma in the context of on-the-job behaviors, approaches to financial planning, and the pursuit of alternative employment before a layoff.

≈ ≈ ≈

Zephyr Before the Storm

It is essential to have a game plan for any significant life change. It is better to prepare than to leave outcomes to chance. Although there may be notification to workers of forthcoming plant closings, research indicates that there is no correlation between advance notice of a shut down and the time period required to become re-employed. This could mean that employees wait for an invitation of employment instead of being proactive. They lose the advantage of formal advance notice of job loss.

Unionized workers have certain advantages over non-union employees. Some advantages are a contract provision for on-going wage payments for a specified time, transfer privileges, and seniority protection. Outside of such contractual arrangements, employees are at the mercy of management.

ða ða ða

On-the-Job Behavior

We interviewed hundreds of employed people and asked a hypothetical question. If you were in a job that you liked and the pay was satisfactory, what actions might you take to prolong your employment after learning of a forthcoming major layoff. The list that follows, Table 6-1, illustrates the order of frequency of actions that employees might take to extend their time on the job. Although we do not consider this list with any sequence significance, we find the suggested courses of action quite interesting.

Table 6-1
ACTIONS TO EXTEND EMPLOYMENT WHEN LAYOFF IS IMMINENT

> Demonstrate loyalty on the job through positive actions
> Don't let the news negatively affect your work ethic
> Check with your manager for truth about the rumors and check on job security
> Offer to work overtime when needed
> Show more initiative, do things that you are not asked to do, but need to be done
> Get to work early, stay late, give 110%
> Learn new jobs to make yourself more valuable to the company
> Find ways for the company to save money
> Demonstrate leadership and help others to get their work done
> Don't complain about the hours or the pay
> Avoid the troublemakers and complainers
> Try to come up with practices that may help to avoid any layoffs
> Don't schedule a vacation during the company's turbulent periods
> Network with the upper management levels
> Look into earning credentials such as software certifications

- Don't try hard to impress, but work hard enough to make an impression
- Get involved in matrix management projects whenever possible
- Don't display hostility when your best friend is fired
- Bargain for a pay and/or benefit cut to avoid a layoff
- Be innovative; bring new ideas to the table
- Maintain a business as usual attitude, but prepare for a next move while confiding in no one

---

Of course, each situation is unique and every person must act as his or her circumstance dictates.

Scenario 6-1

It Worked For Me: Client Case

A 37 year old plant manager reported that, "it didn't look good." Sales were down. Earnings were down. His management team spoke of layoffs. It was a lifo system with employees—Last in First Out. The plant workers liked their jobs. Our client had seniority and no problem for now. But he was unsure how long a business recovery would take. We discussed the possibility of a shorter workweek.

There was a strong likelihood, that if things went as presently headed the company would shut its doors. A group of employees met, and our client suggested that rather than have immediate layoffs, each person agree to go to a 4-day workweek. Everyone agreed with the suggestion because this action would protect the newer employees and provide all with some room to plan for the future.

Prepare for a Soft Landing When a Layoff is Imminent

This plan would reduce costs for the company and retain jobs. Management agreed to the proposal and all employees were placed on an 80% workweek.

Payroll costs were correspondingly reduced in accordance with the plan. Employees were assured of at least three months work with a 20% pay cut. All parties were OK with the change.

Our client viewed the day off as an opportunity to job search. Others did the same. Some took a part-time job to make up the 20% pay loss. Overall, employees had a chance to rest, relax, and wait and/or aggressively pursue other full-time employment. Our client was fortunate to land a job with a government agency with a pay increase over his last job and now he has a much better benefit plan.

Within a year, the troubled plant shut down. The transition period of going to a 4-day workweek was truly a blessing. It worked for many.

Scenario 6-2

Scary Wednesdays: Client Case

A new extreme of job stress was offered by an employee of a telecommunications company who was searching for another job with a different company.

A young woman revealed that the announcement of a layoff was made in late December, to be effective sometime in February. Tensions were high, but the layoff never happened.

The rumor mill started to circulate that the layoff was now going to occur sometime in March.

Lips were sealed as to which departments were going to be affected, and who exactly, was going to be victimized by top management and their insatiable appetites for higher stock prices. The supervisors could offer no support, as they were unsure of their own destiny.

As the days passed in March, more information made its way through the cracks of secrecy. Ash Wednesday was designated as the announcement day. It was to be feared! When the day arrived, everyone seemed to be paralyzed into inaction. No one wanted to be a victim.

The employee informed us that 10:00 a.m., each Wednesday, was the dreaded hour and day. Every Wednesday, employees waited in silence for the telephone ring or for the cold in-person request to proceed down the hall to a secluded office.

Co-workers would exit; their faces stiff and pale. Who would be next? The tension would mount for several hours each dreadful Wednesday. The supervisors would receive word around 1:00 p.m. that all notifications of layoffs were over for the week.

Scary Wednesday's are tough. Her job search engine is in high gear.

❧ ❧ ❧

A Note on Education

Education counts and education pays. In addition to your privately funded continuing education, sign on for as much training or college tuition reimbursement as you can. Get as much education as the company allows. Complete certifications, earn credentials, and be sure to obtain documentation for any internal training programs. Some examples of frequently offered training programs follow.

Table 6-2
JOB TRAINING OFFERED BY MOST ORGANIZATIONS

> Occupational Safety Training
> Employee Health and Wellness Training
> Awareness Training, (various topics)
> Communications
> Quality Control
> Management Training
> Professional and Technical Skills
> Customer Relations
> On-the-job Training

Most employers will include a letter or certificate upon completion of formal or informal training. Be sure to keep copies as documentation.

Another Note on Education

The unemployment rate in 1998 and median earnings by level of education according to the U.S. Bureau of Statistics follows.

Table 6-3
CORRELATION OF:

Unemployment Rate %	Education Level	Median $ Earnings
1.3	Professional Degree	72,700
1.4	Doctorate	62,400
1.6	Master's Degree	50,000
1.9	Bachelor's Degree	40,100
2.5	Associate's Degree	31,700
3.2	Some college	30,400
4.0	High School graduate	26,000

Professional specialty occupations are projected to add the most jobs through year 2008, 5.3 million jobs according to the Bureau of Labor Statistics. The next largest segment for growth is service workers. The two groups are on exact opposite ends of the education level and income level. The gap in education level and earnings potential is widening. This trend is not expected to change.

୧ଈ ୧ଈ ୧ଈ

Surviving the First Round

Remember, "trouble makers" are usually the first to go. It makes life easier for the "stayers" or survivors and management.

Facts are essential. To gather additional facts, you may want to follow reports in the various media where you can learn of pending moves, mergers, EPA violations, union and/or non-union workforce problems. Other actions may be to read stockholders' annual and quarterly reports, if available, in order to remain informed about financial stability.

Demonstrate loyalty through actions such as staying late if necessary, being positive, and by avoiding serial complainers.

A resume is a necessary tool for employment. Write one. Keep it current. This document is your advocate; it is your in-print spokesperson. Emphasize achievements and state-of-the-art training wherever relevant.

There is no law against seeking another job. You are a free agent. Of course, you should be discreet, but inquiries are not a shameful act.

Generally, rumors have some truth, but the truth may be grossly distorted. Care should be taken to discount rumors. However, fact finding as mentioned earlier is a good idea to confirm the elements of truth in the rumors.

If you decide to adopt one or more of the earlier suggested courses of action, that may be the start of your game plan. However, the game plan must be complemented with an economic reality check, just in case you will be out of work for awhile. Table 6-4, outlines the points to consider as a general approach, since the specifics of financial planning were discussed earlier in Chapter 3.

Tightening the Financial Belt

We can learn from others who have been in a financially tight situation and have had to make tough choices. The comments that follow were from respondents to a survey of people who were laid off.

Table 6-4
TOUGH CHOICES

> There was no full-time work available, so I had to work two or sometimes three part-time jobs.
> My spouse had to go to work leaving the kids with relatives, while I work on a contingency basis.
> I virtually eliminated my discretionary spending- no restaurants, movies, or vacations.
> I made a big mistake and maxed out all of my credit cards to buy needed items.
> We borrowed much more than we should have. The interest clock is still running.
> We cut way back on food and clothing.
> I had to compromise the quality of my lifestyle.
> We were forced to apply for Medicaid, since we have no insurance coverage.

Some advice when confronted with financial constraints follows in table 6-5.

Table 6-5
THE DO'S AND DON'TS OF TIGHTENING THE FINANCIAL EXPENDITURES BELT

DO'S
- Prepare and use budgets
- Avoid credit card usage
- Avoid discretionary spending
- Give new meaning to the word frugal
- Seek alternative employment
- Maintain your pragmatic sense of humor

DON'TS
- Ignore the seriousness of the situation
- Wait too long to prepare an action plan
- Pretend everything is the same
- Forget to take time out

A budget is a formal listing of your sources of income and each of your expenses. Be realistic with estimates. Consult with your checkbook to see where your money goes. Refer to Chapter 3 for a model that enables you to look at unemployment in the context of "The Way It Is" and "The Way It Must Be," until all is returned to a steady state. This is a disciplined approach to a reality check.

Credit cards are instruments of evil, if used inappropriately. Usage should be for emergency purposes only. Most credit cards offer exorbitant interest rates, obscene late payment penalties, and high annual fees. Some credit card companies give loan sharks a good name.

Avoid discretionary spending. Even if you have discretionary income, treat it as money to save until potential financial trouble passes you by. Change your lifestyle to getting by without the theater, expensive dinners, unnecessary travel, or spending on luxury items.

Redefine frugality. You don't have to squeeze the nickel, but be on guard. Old habits are tough to change. Readjust as you know you must. Remember it is just for an interim period. Use your budget; circumstances are not the same. Don't forget what could happen if the other shoe drops.

Seek alternative employment if a layoff appears inevitable. You may consider a variety of options for an interim period if you are not fortunate enough to have another job to walk into. Independent contractors work freelance and may work through an agent or alone. Most independent contractors are satisfied with their employment arrangements as long as they have a sufficient amount of work. Another option is on-call workers. This is based on receiving a call to work on an as needed basis. People in this category are not as satisfied with their arrangement as independent contractors. After all, it is less predictable. Temporary help, or agency workers, are paid by the agency whether or not their jobs are temporary. Some jobs have a "permanent" function as mentioned in Chapter 5. Contract firms provide workers and charge a fee per person. Such firms maintain all of the employees on their payroll. Any of the aforementioned plans have minimal, if any benefits, other than pay for the employee.

In general, according to the Department of Labor, about half of contingent workers would prefer to have permanent jobs rather than temporary, about 40% are satisfied, and the remainder indifferent.

Other options may be outsourcing, consulting, or starting your own business. Outsourcing is practiced by many midsize and large companies. The objective of the company is to have a reliable source of supply for various products without carrying the burden of a payroll to produce these products. It is cost efficient for the company, and outsourcing may evolve into a lucrative contract for former employees.

Some current or former employees are asked to stay on or return to the company as a consultant. The pay may be higher than it was as an employee, but there will be no benefits other than the fees.

As discussed earlier in the book, you may want to start your own business as an interim venture or as a permanent enterprise. Refer to Chapter 5 for reference to small business start-up as an alternative.

If you believe that you should treat your situation seriously, then you probably have a sense of imminent danger. It would be logical to prepare an action plan before the fact.

The last person in the world you want to deceive is yourself. Be realistic about what fact based outcomes lie ahead.

Keep your sense of humor. You are taking a proactive stance. You are an action committee. Your alternatives are in place. It's OK to take time out from the sense of urgency—it's a healthy thing to do. You'll get through whatever comes your way.

Perhaps it is a good idea to consider the fact that life-long employment may have been a great concept of yesteryear, but today we do things quite differently.

The current wisdom on employment is to consider yourself self-employed, even if you are working for a large company with all the benefits. When you have that concept of self-employment, you are always on the lookout for the next opportunity. You are keeping your training and education up to date. You continue networking. You review and revise your resume at least annually.

There was a hospital administrator who yearly went on a job interview. He would generate options and then decide if he really wanted to stay in his current job, after looking at others. He always had a realistic idea about salaries and job availability. He considered it part of his life long career planning process.

Scenario 6-3

Early Notification: Client Case

A large manufacturing plant was closing and relocating. Employees were given about 18 months notification. They had to decide if they wanted to move their families to the new location. There was no promise of the same job, only that they would be hired if they chose to stay on. Predictably, many started looking for jobs locally. With many two career families, moving was a problem for most. Others just hunkered down and were willing to wait and see. One of the managers, who had been with the company for 20 years, decided this was a great time for all kinds of changes. A new place to live sounded exciting. His wife was self-employed and believed that she might have more advantages in the new and larger city. But he was bored doing the same kind of engineering for so many years.

The company was just beginning their ISO program. With his management and engineering background, and his seniority, he volunteered to work with the new ISO project. This would require that he travel weekly to the new location, working with staff in both plants. Although it sounded hectic initially, he was able to check on real estate options, look at a variety of neighborhoods, and find out some information about his wife's options. All this information was gathered long before the move. As a consequence, he was able to locate housing at a good price, before all the other relocated employees moved to the area in search of scarce housing. He and his wife actually felt somewhat settled in their new home shortly after the move because of the earlier preparations.

He became a more valuable employee. Further, he was able to enrich his own career with new work and challenges. He was integrated into the new team before he had to move. There were many tangible as well as intangible benefits with his choice to move in a new direction. In addition, he had a chance to introduce himself to the new environment.

Early notification can be a gift if used properly.

Scenario 6-4

Divine Intervention: Client Case

A large religious institution was planning a merger with two other smaller affiliated groups. The organization decided that on a certain date, each would go out of existence and a new organization would be formed. This meant that every employee, with the exception of parish staff, would have to re-apply for new positions. The transition period was two and one half years. A national program series of career transition workshops were offered to all employees of all levels. So this group of workers had lots of time to prepare. It was interesting to watch the differing reactions to the announcement. The most successful folks were those who had attended the workshops, completed the assignments on self-assessment, and continued to do good work.

The Career Transition program generated many new jobs in the organization during the last 30 months. One of the secretaries volunteered to manage all the scheduling of the workshops and attendees, direct all the transfer of materials, maintain communications with the consultants, and monitor the feeding and housing needs of all the participants. She had always loved planning and running special events for her church and her big annual family reunions. She never really loved her clerical work, but saw it as service to the church. And now her church might put her out of work!

So the opportunity to do something she loved and had the skills and experience for (in the volunteer arena) allowed her to continue service to her church. It seemed perfect. She made a proposal to her boss initially and then to the program director and eventually landed the job. She performed with great delight and competence. Her skills of handling many details at once and negotiating with suppliers allowed for the smooth production of the residential workshops.

She stayed employed right up to the last day. This task gave her the first opportunity to manage other workers.

Her accomplishments allowed her to create an entirely new resume. She listed the clerical skills that supported her planning and organizational abilities. Of course, once the merger was complete, there was no need in the new church organization for her skills. Armed with the new resume, letters of commendation from all levels of the organization, and her confidence based on success, she landed a job as a special events coordinator with a hotel chain. There she worked with managers of training programs that were conducted at the hotel.

Having the courage to speak up about what you love doing, even if you have never been paid for it can move you in a career direction with success. Early notification allows you to try out some new behaviors, to be of greater value and service to the organization.

Early announcement of closings can be a true gift of time. In the case of the church merger discussed earlier, many of the employees took advantage of a tuition reimbursement program that they had ignored previously. Many employees finished degree programs that they had begun earlier. Others chose to take workshops and seminars to more fully develop existing skills. These additional credentials boosted their resumes and provided them with more confidence in the job search.

❧ ❧ ❧

Job Search Assistance

Your job search may include a variety of approaches such as headhunters, placement agencies, networking, internet searches, or some combination of two or more.

For your reference a listing of some of the more popular internet job search addresses are provided in Table 6-6.

Table 6-6
More Job Search Web Addresses

www.

ajb.dni.us
career.com
employmentguide.com
gojobs.com
headhunter.com
hotjobs.com
jobs.com
monster.com
net-temps.com
thingamajob.com

Be sure to make hard copies of solid leads during your job search. One of these documents might put you right on target!

Chapter Seven

PULL IT ALL TOGETHER

A Recapitulation

Introduction

We will look at planning for change, in the context of two major forces: the internal and the external environments of your life and your lifestyle. Remember, planning is preparing, and tomorrow will always become today.

Navigating Through the Perils

A good place to begin with safeguarding what you have is to assess who you really are, how you got where you are, and where you intend to go. Unless someone simply handed you all of your assets, chances are good that you earned them. You earned what you have based on your past efforts and maybe some luck. There are forces always at play in our lives. Some call these forces coincidence, others call them divine intervention. Whatever the label, things change, sometimes for better and sometimes for worse.

The internal environment includes factors over which you have a large amount of control. For example, you have control over how you spend your money. Whether or not you take control or let it be siphoned away is another matter. You have control over how you spend your leisure time. Some people opt to use their spare time in pursuit of more education, perhaps working toward an advanced degree or updating their computer skills. At the other extreme, some choose to overdose on rest and relaxation.

The external environment includes forces over which you have little influence and no control. For example, you have no control over the rate of inflation, the economy, or the impact of international competition for jobs and factory locations. You may or may not have some influence over an organization's decision to downsize, but certainly no control over such a high level decision.

We will examine a series of meaningful internal environmental factors. This examination will reveal ways as to how you may exercise control and how you might strengthen your overall economic and lifestyle position for the present and for the future.

There is a resource center at the end of this chapter. It includes checklists and tables that appear throughout the book. Each is cross-referenced to its respective chapter. This format will enable you to envision the big picture of your current situation. It will also serve as channel markers to keep you on course as you progress on your journey.

A Safe Harbor

Who are you? After exchanging names, one of the first questions asked when you meet someone for the first time is, "what do you do?" In the United States, we tend to associate "what you do" with "who you are." After all, your education and your job are the two prime indicators of social status in the U.S. Let's consider a sort of resume type checklist to answer the question, "Who are you"? You may want to write responses to the questions that follow. This could prove to be a very worthwhile exercise.

Education
What occupational credentials do you hold?
What certifications do you hold?
What licenses do you hold?
What college degrees do you hold?
What college degrees are you working toward?
What professional designations do you have?
What advanced training courses or programs have you completed?

Work Experience
If employed, what is your current job title? Job duties? Former job titles? Former job duties?
If unemployed, what were your former job titles? Job duties?
How would you demonstrate advancement in your job area in terms of progressive responsibility?

How would you demonstrate that your writing skills are at an appropriate level for your job?

How would you describe your interpersonal skills? Would your co-workers past or present agree?

How would you describe your leadership qualities? Would your co-workers past or present agree?

How do you handle conflict in the workplace?

Personal Attributes

How would you describe the internal motivating forces that drive you on the job? Off the job?

Have you served in volunteer organizations? In what role?

Have you served as an officer in a trade or professional organization?

Professional/Technical Growth

What have you done lately?

How have you updated your job skills?

What publications do you read that are related to your job area?

When did you last attend a conference or seminar related to concerns in your industry?

Leisure Activities

What do you do for fun?

What do you do for mental and physical fitness?

Goals
Where do you expect to be in 5 years?
How do you plan to get there?
Where do you expect to be in 10 years?
How do you plan to get there?

Now that you've had a chance to reflect on your past, present, and future, let's frame your thoughts into a review of both your internal and external environments.

A checklist of internal environmental threats, opportunities, and proposed courses of action follows. The format includes consideration of:

Income Level
Adaptability
Health
Spending Habits
Retirement Planning
Dependents
Cost of Living
Debt Structure
Education

As a demonstration of how to use this checklist an example is provided, using the case of Ben Hirt. A blank copy appears in the resource center at the end of this chapter.

Ben Hirt was recently "downsized." He has a job offer that is similar to his former job, but with 15% less pay. He has decided to accept the job, but has to think through the full impact of this change. Ben examined his internal environment, determined where he is, and what he must do to truly take control and plan for the future.

INTERNAL ENVIRONMENT ANALYSIS AND ACTION PLAN FOR:
Ben Hirt

Item: Income Level

Threats:
Too low, no increase, reduction in pay, layoff

Opportunities:
Acquire a better job, higher pay, and better job security

Proposed course of action:
Cross-train for other work, take college courses, earn a professional credential, take tests required for a license

Item: Adaptability

Threats:
Antiquated job skills

Opportunities:
Job advancement

Proposed course of action:
Update job skills and be informed and receptive to new work methods

Item: Health

Threats:
Illness or injury

Opportunities:
Good health assurance activities, leisure activities, and precautions

Proposed course of action:
Have medical checkups, diet wisely and exercise regularly

Item: Spending Habits

Threats:
All disposable dollars are consumed so no discretionary dollars available

Opportunities:
Conserve by living below means and save

Proposed course of action:
Prioritize, budget, budget, and budget, until it works

Item: Retirement Planning

Threats:
Not enough money to maintain current standard of living

Opportunities:
Tax sheltered retirement plans

Proposed course of action:
Investigate and participate in viable programs as much as possible

Item: Dependents

Threats:
Remaining dependent after 24 years of age

Opportunities:
Emancipation, gainfully employed, pay for your lunch on occasion

Proposed course of action:
Encouragement, counseling on how to achieve independence

Item: Cost of Living

Threats:
Increases

Opportunities:
   Pay plan tied to inflation

Proposed course of action:
   Inquire before hire, serve on contract negotiation committee, if an option

Item: Debt Structure
Threats:
   Too much debt

Opportunities:
   Reduce interest costs and monthly payments

Proposed course of action:
   Consolidate debt by refinancing, stop use of credit cards for discretionary items

Item: Education
Threats:
   Not enough, inappropriate

Opportunities:
   Use education as a competitive edge

Proposed course of action:
   Take courses, learn new software packages

Next, we will examine a series of external environmental factors for Ben Hirt, in terms of how to keep abreast of forthcoming change and prepare for the inevitable—more change. Also, we will discuss how one might integrate choices from the internal environment with the outside world, thereby enhancing probability of overall economic and lifestyle success.

External forces contain threats and opportunities. It is up to you to sort these out. Indeed, a wise individual

Pull It All Together

will shore up his or her weaknesses to overcome threats or potential threats and capitalize on opportunities.

A checklist of external environmental threats, opportunities, and proposed courses of action for Ben Hirt follows. The format includes consideration of:

> Job
> Foreign Competition
> Re-engineering Jobs
> Economy
> Industry Trends

A blank copy of the analysis appears in the resource center at the end of this chapter.

EXTERNAL ENVIRONMENT ANALYSIS AND ACTION PLAN FOR:
Ben Hirt

Item: Job

Threats:
> Demotion, elimination, transfer, outplacement

Opportunities:
> Promotion, lateral transfer, relocate, become an independent contractor

Proposed course of action:
> Train, perform well, document successes, follow the official company news and the grapevine, prepare for a transfer, consider working as an independent contractor

Item: Foreign Competition

Threats:
> Jobs going overseas, foreign business gaining larger market share

Opportunities:
> Lower prices, after-market products and services may increase in the U.S., many foreign companies are building manufacturing facilities in the U.S. that will provide jobs

Proposed course of action:
> Keep current with mergers and buyouts, announcements of new plants by foreign business, consider a job overseas, if feasible

Item: Re-engineering Jobs

Threats:
> Work tasks are automated, job is exported, job is redundant and then eliminated

Opportunities:
> Job enrichment, a fine tuned job may offer better job security

Proposed course of action:
> Reengineer own job description and duties to show better efficiency

Item: Economy

Threats:
> Inflation, unemployment, more taxes

Opportunities:
> Methodical shopping, seek job classes in demand, use tax shelters

Proposed course of action:
> Bargain shop, read job market reports, learn more about tax shelters to protect assets

Item: Industry Trends

Threats:
More automation and use of industrial robots

Opportunities:
New jobs are created especially in the fields of programming, electronics, mechanical technologies and the service sector

Proposed course of action:
Retrain, cross-train, if job phase out is imminent, start preparing now

❧ ❧ ❧

What Lies Ahead?

Red skies at night or red skies in the morn? As with the weather, the only certainty is change. A barometer may help forecast change. Why not create your own barometer to forecast change in the workplace? Some of the resources from which to collect data for your "customized" barometer follow. You could use association publications, seminars, conferences, government reports and publications, newspaper accounts of job creation or job elimination, industry trends, networking, reading about new technologies, and closely following the current events of the global marketplace.

❧ ❧ ❧

The Biggest Job Market Threats

We can count on more and more automation. As technology grows it expands its influence over the way work gets done. Until recently, the job of secretary was thought of as a permanent fixture in American enterprise. However, the need for this job role diminishes, as it becomes more common for management personnel to use their computers to take care of their own reporting, business correspondence, and other clerical tasks. Soon the workplace will have more sophisticated voice control document generators with edit features and no keystrokes required.

Our newspaper headlines continue to announce business mergers, which may be cause for celebration for shareholders. The downside of the news is that it will most likely result in layoffs because of redundant jobs. Businesses will "trim-line" operations in order to increase shareholder wealth.

As our global marketplace grows so will opportunities to locate labor factories where per capita income is extremely low. Not only is it attractive to export jobs, but also to make huge capital investment commitments in foreign countries, such as China, where there is potential for exponential market growth.

Forecasted Job Opportunities

It is always a tough call to state what's hot and what's not for any distance into the future, because of the unpredictability of technological and other environmental change. However, the U.S. Department of Labor forecasters see growth and/or stability in certain job titles that were listed in Chapter 3.

Employee Compensation:
Table 7-1 lists the current average wages for different occupational groups. Trends indicate that this relative pattern of variance among occupational groups will persist.

Table 7-1
What Employers Pay Per Hour
Including Benefits
Bureau of Labor Statistics – March 2001

Occupational Group

White-collar occupations	$26.82
Professional specialty and technical	36.04
Professional specialty	38.77
Nurses	32.26
Teachers	40.93
Technical	26.97
Executive, administrative, and managerial	40.25
Administrative support, including clerical	17.59
Blue-collar occupations	19.57
Service occupations	12.40

Summary:
All is contingent on where you are and where you would like to be. Chances are good that you will not only go through several job changes, but career changes as well. In order to best prepare for change, be adaptable.

Have a back up plan. Research and find your best opportunities before the storm, not during or after. You can turn sweaty palms into a firm grip.

Contingency plans can be privately kept by you. You needn't reveal your strategy to others. You may never use your contingency plan, but clearly it is better to have it and not to need it, than to need it and not to have it. Be sure to use the resource center at the end of this chapter. It will guide you through the planning process.

Resource Center

This section serves as a recapitulation of the checklists and tables that appear throughout the book. You may use these resources with a cafeteria style approach. Pick a topic and choose a form to accommodate your needs.

Table of Contents

1. Cash Budget (from Chapter 3)
   The Way It Is With Unemployment

2. Cash Budget (from Chapter 3)
   The Way It Must Be—Bridging the Gap

3. You as the Product (from Chapter 4)
   Self-Analysis Checklist

4. Self-Promotion (from Chapter 4)
   Windows of Opportunity Checklist

5. New Place (from Chapter 4)
   New Place Checklist

6. Worksheet for Compensation Package Analysis (from Chapter 4)
   Checklist for Determining Your Price

7. Checklist of Addresses on the World Wide Web for Major Job Banks (from Chapter 4)

8. Internal Environment (from Chapter 7)
   Analysis and Action Plan

9. External Environment (from Chapter 7)
   Analysis and Action Plan

1. Cash Budget (from Chapter 3)

These worksheets are for analysis of your financial situation. You may expand or in other ways modify the budget worksheets. For a comprehensive review of the budget process, refer to Chapter 3.

Cash Budget
The Way It Is
<u>With Unemployment</u>

Month by Month   Totals

Revenue—After Tax
  Salary 1
  Salary 2
  Interest Income
  Other Sources of Funds
  Total Revenue

Disbursements
  Mortgage
  Automobile Loan
  Groceries
  Utilities
  Clothing
  Home Furnishings
  Home Improvements
  Insurance Life
  Insurance Other
  Tuition
  Entertainment
  Credit Cards
  Memberships
  Publications
  Donations
  Other

Total Disbursements
Excess or (Shortage)

Pull It All Together

2. Cash Budget (from Chapter 3)

Cash Budget
The Way It Must Be
Bridging the Gap

                                    Month by Month   Totals

Revenue—After Tax
   Salary 1
   Salary 2
   Interest Income
   Other Sources of Funds
   Total Revenue

Disbursements
   Mortgage
   Automobile Loan
   Groceries
   Utilities
   Clothing
   Home Furnishings
   Home Improvements
   Insurance Life
   Insurance Other
   Tuition
   Entertainment
   Credit Cards
   Memberships
   Publications
   Donations
   Other

Total Disbursements
Excess or (Shortage)

3. You as the Product (from Chapter 4)

You may view yourself as a product into which prospective employers may want to invest. Review what you have to offer and accentuate the positive!

You as the "Product" Self-Analysis Checklist

Education	Physical Limitations
Experience	Interpersonal Skills
Availability	Appearance
Reliability	Special Skills

---

4. Self-Promotion (from Chapter 4)

Consider the options that are listed below in the context of how you might best capitalize on your promotional opportunities. Prepare an action plan so that you are sure to follow through and effectively promote yourself.

**Self-Promotion
Windows of Opportunity Checklist**

Personal Selling	**Public Relations**
Networking	Announcements
Associations	Business Cards
	Volunteer Work
Advertising	
Resume	**Generating Options**
Cover Letter	Placement Tests
Letters of Inquiry	World Wide Web Inquiries
Headhunters	Transition Center Services
	Organizations of Specific Groups

Pull It All Together

5. New Place (from Chapter 4)

If relocating is in the wind, as an option or necessity, you may want to run through at least some of the questions that follow.

Questions to Answer for A New Place Decision—Checklist

Can I commute rather than relocate?

What about my spouse's job and income?

How will the move impact upon the kids, (school, friends, activities, etc.)?

How good are the schools at the new location?

Is the cost of living more or less where the new job is located?

What is the tax structure? How will it impact upon my overall cost of living?

What is the quality of living compared to where I am now?

What is the predominant life style—urban, suburban, rural, country?

Is there a degree in progress for me or my spouse? Can it be finished without a residency?

How are the overall employment opportunities in the geographic area under consideration?

Are quality day care facilities available? At what cost?

Are there services conveniently located—shopping centers, grocery stores, etc.?

Are there adequate health care facilities for my family's needs?

What is the primary transportation system?

How much will the relocation cost? Who will pay?

Is the weather dramatically different from what I am accustomed to?

What kind of culture will I have to become acclimated to?

6. Worksheet for Compensation Package Analysis (from Chapter 4)

Your "price" is the amount of dollars and benefits that you are willing to accept in exchange for your services. You can and should analyze the total value of the compensation package in order to compare one offer with another. The worksheet that follows gives you a framework for such an analysis.

Worksheet for Compensation Package Analysis
Annualized Value

Item	Former Job	New Job	Variance
Salary			
Overtime			
Health Care			
Cost of Living Increases			
Retirement Plan			
Education Reimbursement			
Vacation Time			
Personal Time			
Transportation Reimbursement			
Living Expenses			
Day Care			
Relocation Payments			
Cafeteria Benefits Plan			
Retrenchment Plan			
Other			
Total Value of Compensation Package			

7. Checklist of Addresses on the World Wide Web For Major Job Banks (from Chapter 4)

Here is a valuable resource to conduct a job search using your computer (or one at a transition center or library). You may "design" your search criteria, contingent on the Web site, specifying the parameters of the job for which you are searching. For example, you may indicate the type of work you are interested in and the geographic location where you would like to work.

Checklist of Addresses on the World Wide Web for the Major Job Banks

America's Employers
www.americasemployers.com

America's Job Bank
www.ajb.dni.us

Career.Com
www.career.com

Career Mosaic
www.careermosaic.com

College Grad
www.collegegrad.com

Department of Labor
www.doleta.gov

Employment Guide
www.employmentguide.com

Go Jobs
www.gojobs.com

Head Hunter
www.headhunter.net

Hot Jobs
www.hotjobs.com

Job Options
www.joboptions.com

Jobs
www.jobs.com

Job Star
www.jobstar.com

Monster Board
www.monster.com

Net Temps
www.net-temps.com

ThingamaJob
www.thingamajob.com

Pull It All Together

8. Internal Environment (from Chapter 7)

This is your environment. You should exercise control over these factors whenever possible. The purpose of this exercise is to establish an action plan to take control and get into forward motion. An example of a person using this worksheet was given earlier in the chapter.

Personal Checklist of Internal Environmental Threats, Opportunities, and Proposed Courses of Action

Item	Threats	Opportunities	Proposed Course of Action
Income level			
Adaptability			
Health			
Spending Habits			
Retirement Planning			
Dependents			
Cost of Living			
Debt Structure			
Education			

9. External Environment (from Chapter 7)

These forces exist around you and certainly impact upon you. Although you have no control over these factors, you should be well aware of the current events in your industry and, in particular, your company. An example of a person being in touch and dealing with his external environment was given earlier in the chapter.

Personal Checklist of External Environmental Threats, Opportunities, and Proposed Courses of Action

Item	Threats	Opportunities	Proposed Course of Action
Job			
Foreign Competition			
Re-engineering Jobs			
Economy			
Industry Trends			

The prime purpose of this book is to reassure the reader that he or she can work through troubled times. There are rough seas and rough times. Sometimes few choices exist when circumstances dictate direction. We have compiled these resources to help you sort out all possible viable options. Use as needed!

❧ ❧ ❧

Epilogue

SOME FINAL THOUGHTS

There is a myriad of details and issues to deal with throughout the journey of life. We know of no roadmap or directions for a completely smooth ride. However, we hope our book has provided some helpful guidance for your journey through your life-career. We have drawn on the experiences of many people who have found the ways and means to survive and thrive in spite of obstacles.

Carving out a living is not an easy task even when well prepared. We hope our book will serve as a steering mechanism through your charted course.

We wish you every success and happiness on your career path. We know that you will enrich your life and the lives of others around you when you are working with your very best skills, acknowledging and honoring your highest values and enjoying yourself in the process. We hope the path you travel and the choices you make are mutually compatible.

Best wishes for a healthy and prosperous journey!

Richard J. Van Ness and Edith M. Donohue

About the Authors

Richard J. Van Ness, Ph.D. is professor of management and finance. He serves as a mentor to career changing adult students. He is a management consultant and has written several books on finance, business start-up, and professional development. In an earlier career, Dr. Van Ness was the controller of an international construction company.

ea ea ea

Edith M. Donohue, Ph.D., is a Human Resource consultant with over 20 years experience in career transition services. She worked with many large companies providing outplacement advice and workshops to employees. She also works with individuals seeking career change. In an earlier career, Dr. Donohue was Associate Professor of Human Resource Development in a graduate program for adult students.